Primary 4A
Preface

Primary Mathematics Intensive Practice is a series of 12 books written to provide challenging supplementary material for Singapore's Primary Mathematics,

The primary objective of this series of books is to help students generate greater interest in mathematics and gain more confidence in solving mathematical problems. To achieve this, special features are incorporated in the series.

SPECIAL FEATURES

Topical Review
Enables students of mixed abilities to be exposed to a good variety of questions which are of varying levels of difficulty so as to help them develop a better understanding of mathematical concepts and their applications.

Mid-Year or End-Of-Year Review
Provides students with a good review that summarizes the topics learned in Primary Mathematics.

Take the Challenge!
Deepens students' mathematical concepts and helps develop their mathematical reasoning and higher-order thinking skills as they practice their problem-solving strategies.

More Challenging Problems
Stimulate students' interest through challenging and thought-provoking problems which encourage them to think critically and creatively as they apply their knowledge and experience in solving these problems.

Why this Series?
Students will find this series of books a good complement and supplement to the Primary Mathematics textbooks and workbooks. The comprehensive coverage certainly makes this series a valuable resource for teachers, parents and tutors.

It is hoped that the special features in this series of books will inspire and spur young people to achieve better mathematical competency and greater mathematics problem-solving skills.

Published by
SingaporeMath.com Inc
404 Beavercreek Road #225
Oregon City, OR 97045
U.S.A.
E-mail: customerservice@singaporemath.com
www.singaporemath.com

First published 2004
Reprinted 2005
Reprinted 2007

ISBN 1-932906-06-1

Printed in Singapore

Our special thanks to Jenny Hoerst for her assistance in editing the U.S. edition of
Primary Mathematics Intensive Practice.

Avinash

Primary 4A
Contents

Topic 1: Whole Numbers

1. Each of the following represents a numeral. Write it in figures and then in words. The first one has been done for you.

	Ten Thousands	Thousands	Hundreds	Tens	Ones
(a)		★★★	★★★★★★★	★★	★★★★★★
(b)	★★★★		★★	★★★★★★	★★★
(c)	★★★		★★★★	★★	★
(d)	★	★★		★★★★	★★★★★

★ stands for 1 unit in each respective place value.

(a) ___3726___

   Three thousand, seven hundred twenty-six

(b) _____

   _____

(c) _____

   _____

(d) _____

   _____

2. Write the following in numerals.

   (a) Forty-three thousand, two hundred five

   _____

(b)   Seventy thousand, six hundred

_____

(c)   Eight thousand, three hundred ninety-eight dollars

$_____

(d)   Twenty thousand, seven dollars

$_____

3.   Write the following in words.

   (a)   20,940

   _____

   (b)   49,267

   _____

   (c) $73,008

   _____

   (d) $90,909

   _____

4.   Complete the number pattern in the cross-number puzzle.

	78,320	78,420		78,620
	68,320			78,619
56,320	57,320		59,320	
	48,320			
				78,616
	28,310	28,320	28,330	
27,300				
25,300				
24,300				

5. Fill in the blanks.

   (a) $87,434 = 80,000 +$ _____ $+ 400 + 30 + 4$

   (b) $53,040 = 50,000 + 3000 +$ _____ $+ 40$

   (c) $30,000 + 7000 +$ _____ $+ 20 + 3 = 37,623$

   (d) _____ $+ 6000 + 200 + 10 + 9 = 86,219$

   (e) _____ $= 20,000 + 3000 + 400 + 70 + 8$

   (f) $49,703 = 40,000 + 9000 + 700 +$ _____

6. Fill in the blanks.

   (a) _____ is 1 less than 9999.

   (b) 7635 is 10 less than _____.

   (c) _____ is 100 less than 89,093.

   (d) 18,740 is 1000 less than _____.

   (e) _____ is 10,000 less than 91,362.

   (f) _____ is 1 more than 99,999.

   (g) 5632 is 10 more than _____.

   (h) _____ is 100 more than 13,131.

   (i) 69,696 is 1000 more than _____.

   (j) _____ is 10,000 more than 32,004.

7. Arrange these numbers in increasing order.

   (a) 18,080; 1080; 10,088; 18,008

   _____

   (b) 36,071; 4931; 50,218; 76,732

   _____

8. Arrange these numbers in decreasing order.

(a) 69,996; 6996; 9669; 96,669

_____

(b) 58,104; 75,091; 2033; 100,000

_____

9. Write the value of each bold digit in each of the following numerals. Then fill in the blank that follows.

(a)

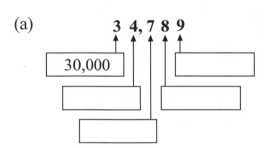

3 4, 7 8 9

30,000

The value of the digit '4' is _____ more than the value of the digit '8'.

(b)

6 9, 9 9 6

The value of the digit '9' in the tens place is _____ less than the value of the digit '9' in the thousands place.

(c)

7 3, 0 4 3

There are _____ tens in the value of the digit '3' in the thousands place.

(d)

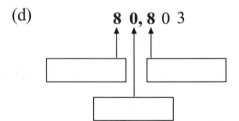

8 0, 8 0 3

There are _____ hundreds in the value of the digit '8' in the ten thousands place.

4

10. Do the following.

(a) $3000 \times 3 =$ _____

(b) $5000 \times 7 =$ _____

(c) $12,000 \times 8 =$ _____

(d) $22,000 \times 4 =$ _____

(e) $7000 \times 6 =$ _____

(f) $9000 \div 3 =$ _____

(g) $60,000 \div 5 =$ _____

(h) $56,000 \div 8 =$ _____

(i) $42,000 \div 7 =$ _____

(j) $63,000 \div 9 =$ _____

(k) $14,000 - 8000 =$ _____

(l) $20,000 \div 4 =$ _____

(m) $13,000 \times 6 =$ _____

(n) $47,000 + 5000 =$ _____

(o) $100,000 \div 4 =$ _____

11. Fill in the blanks.

(a) In the numeral **68,349**,

(i) the value of the digit '6' is _____,

(ii) the digit '8' stands for _____,

(iii) the digit '3' is in the _____ place,

(iv) the digit '4' stands for _____ tens,

(v) the value of the digit '9' is _____,

(vi) the sum of the value of the largest digit and the value of the smallest digit is _____,

(vii) the value of the digit '8' is _____ times the value of the digit '4'.

(b)   In the numeral **39,624**,

   (i)   the digit '2' stands for _____,

   (ii)   the value of the digit '4' is _____,

   (iii)   the value of the digit '6' is _____,

   (iv)   the digit '9' is in the _____ place,

   (v)   the digit '3' has a value of _____ ten thousands,

   (vi)   the difference between the value of the largest digit and the value of the smallest digit is _____,

   (vii)   the value of the digit in the ten thousands place is _____ times the value of the digit in the hundreds place.

12.   The table below shows the number of stickers that each boy has. Round each number to the nearest 10 and to the nearest 100.

Boys	Number of stickers	Round to the nearest 10	Round to the nearest 100
Andrew	687		
Martin	1494		
Roland	1005		
Pablo	906		
Samuel	1753		
Jonathan	1999		

13.   Circle all the possible values in each of the following questions.

(a)   The height of a tree is about 180 m when rounded to the nearest ten meters. Which of these could be the actual height of the tree?

   174 m   184 m   179 m   187 m   189 m   181 m

(b) Tom has about $800 when rounded to the nearest $100. Which of the following could be the actual amount of money Tom has?

$745 $780 $895 $850 $805 $819

14. Round each number to the nearest 10 and then estimate the value of each of the following.

Example: 417   +   281
                ↓   ↓
            $\boxed{420}$ + $\boxed{280}$ = $\boxed{700}$

(a) $692 + 319 \approx$ (b) $8428 + 102 \approx$

(c) $875 - 525 \approx$ (d) $1608 - 815 \approx$

(e) $123 + 479 - 305 \approx$ (f) $4811 - 98 - 482 \approx$

(g) $2399 - 188 + 795 \approx$ (h) $994 + 1215 - 392 \approx$

15. Round each number to the nearest 100 and then estimate the value of each of the following.

Example: 417   +   281
                ↓   ↓
            $\boxed{400}$ + $\boxed{300}$ = $\boxed{700}$

(a) $692 + 319 \approx$ (b) $8428 + 102 \approx$

(c) $875 - 525 \approx$ (d) $1608 - 815 \approx$

(e) $123 + 479 - 305 \approx$ (f) $4811 - 98 - 482 \approx$

(g) $2399 - 188 + 795 \approx$ (h) $994 + 1215 - 392 \approx$

16. (a) What do you notice about the estimated values obtained in Questions 14 and 15?

_____

(b) Which estimation method is easier? Rounding to the nearest 10 or to the nearest 100?

_____

17. List all the factors of each of the following numbers systematically.

Example: 18 ⟶ 1 × 18
                  2 × 9
                  3 × 6

The factors of 18 are **1**, **2**, **3**, **6**, **9** and **18**.

(a) 24

The factors of 24 are _____ .

(b) 35

The factors of 35 are _____ .

(c) 52

The factors of 52 are _____ .

(d) 63

The factors of 63 are _____ .

(e) 75

The factors of 75 are _____ .

(f) 81

The factors of 81 are _____ .

(g) 98

The factors of 98 are _____ .

18. Write 'Yes' or 'No' in each of the following. Show your work.

Example: 100 ÷ 4 = 25
100 is exactly divisible by 4
So, 4 is a factor of 100.

(a) Is 3 a factor of 39?

(b) Is 6 a factor of 90?

(c) Is 8 a factor of 92?

(d) Is 4 a factor of 81?

19. (a) Complete the table below by filling in 'Yes' or 'No'.

Number	Is 3 a factor?	Is 4 a factor?	Is 7 a factor?
21			
36			
40			
57			
63			
76			
84			
96			

(b) Which of the number(s) above has/have 3, 4 and 7 as its factors?

(c) If I have 168 rubber bands, can I tie them into 3, 4 or 7 equal bundles? Show your work.

20. Find the common factors of the following pairs of numbers.

   (a) 16 and 24

   $16 \longrightarrow$ ① × 16 $24 \longrightarrow$ ① × 24

   ② × 8   ② × _____

   ④ × _____   3 × _____

                              ④ × _____

   The common factors of 16 and 24 are _____.

   (b)   25 and 45

   The common factors of 25 and 45 are _____.

   (c)   32 and 54

   The common factors of 32 and 54 are _____.

   (d)   39 and 65

   The common factors of 39 and 65 are _____.

21. Refer to your solutions for Question 20 above and answer 'Yes' or 'No' to each of the following.

   (a) Is 3 a common factor of 24 and 54?   _____

   (b) Are both 25 and 65 exactly divisible by 5?   _____

   (c) Are 1 and 13 common factors of 45 and 65?   _____

22. List the first 8 multiples of each number and circle the first, fourth and eighth multiple.

    (a)   3 :

    (b)   7 :

    (c)   8 :

    (d)   12 :

23. Fill in the blanks and find the first two common multiples of each pair of numbers.

    (a)   4 and 6

         Multiples of 4 are 4, 8, _____, _____, _____, _____, _____, ...

         Multiples of 6 are 6, 12, _____, _____, _____, _____, _____, ...

         The first two common multiples of 4 and 6 are _____ and _____.

    (b)   5 and 9

         Multiples of 5 are 40, _____, _____, _____, _____, _____, _____,

         _____, _____, _____, _____, ...

         Multiples of 9 are 36, _____, _____, _____, _____, _____, _____, ...

         The first two common multiples of 5 and 9 are _____ and _____.

    (c)   7 and 6

         Multiples of 7 are _____

         Multiples of 6 are _____

         The first two common multiples of 7 and 6 are _____ and _____.

    (d)   8 and 12

         Multiples of 8 are _____

         Multiples of 12 are _____

         The first two common multiples of 8 and 12 are _____ and _____.

24. Refer to your solutions for Questions 22 and 23 above and answer 'Yes' or 'No' to each of the following.

(a) Is 24 a multiple of 4?

(b) Can you divide 40 by 7?

(c) Is 63 a common multiple of 7 and 8?

(d) A teacher has 42 pens and 56 pencils. She wants to distribute them to her class of 14 preschoolers, such that each child will get the same number of pens and pencils. Is it possible? Show your work.

WORD PROBLEMS

1. Solve these riddles to find out what number I am.
   (a) I am a number between 20 and 30, a multiple of 4 and also a multiple of 7.

   (b) I am a number between 30 and 40. I am a factor of 70.

   (c) I am an odd number smaller than 50 but greater than 30. I am a multiple of 7. I am not a multiple of 5.

(d) I am a number greater than 10 but smaller than 40. I am a factor of 56 but not a multiple of 4.

2. There are 6500 ml of water in a large bucket. I use 3 ℓ 25 ml of it. How many milliliters of water are left in the bucket?

3. On Friday, Mr. Trucker drove 392 mi to Loonytown. On Saturday, he drove 59 mi further than on Friday to Tunetown. What was the total distance he travelled on the two days, to the nearest 100 mi?

4. A duck weighs 3 kg 55 g. A chicken is 415 g lighter than the duck. How much do the duck and chicken weigh altogether?

5. Three pieces of strings are 64 in., 80 in. and 96 in. long. If they are to be cut into shorter pieces of equal length without any wastage or leftover, what is the longest possible length of each equal piece?

6. Winona wants to buy a computer, monitor, and printer that costs $2285. Her father gives her $1080 while her mother gives her $120 less than that given by her father. How much more money does Winona need?

7. (a) Peter has 5610 coins and Paul has 1897 coins. Round the number of coins they have altogether to the nearest hundred.

   (b) If 28 girls have 273 beads each, what is the estimated number of beads they have in total?

8. Mrs. Selvam went shopping with $450. She would like to buy the following items:

a handbag	—	$199
a pair of sandals	—	$69
a coat	—	$139

   (a) Estimate the total cost of these three items.
   Did Mrs. Selvam have enough money to buy all the three items?

   (b) Mrs. Selvam remembered that she needed to buy a birthday gift. She found a television set that cost $168. If Mrs. Selvam had $43 left after buying the three items, estimate the amount of money she would need to buy the television set.

9. Of the 64,000 people who visited an exhibition, 30,450 were men and 18,131 were women. How many more adults than children visited the exhibition?

10. Aisha has $72 and Esther has $56. How much money must Aisha give to Esther so that both of them will have an equal amount of money?

11. Carl collected 165 cards. He realized that he had 21 identical cards and he gave them to Tessa. Now Tessa has 48 cards more than Carl. How many cards did Tessa have at first?

12. Davina, Jean and Nancy have a total savings of $4800. If Davina saves $480 more than Nancy and Jean saves $330 less than Davina, how much does Jean save?

13. Mr. Ching wants to give a group of his violin students some reward stickers. If he gives each student 3 stickers, he will have 75 stickers left. If he gives each student 6 stickers, he will need 30 more stickers.
    (a) How many students are there in Mr. Ching's violin group?
    (b) How many reward stickers does he have?

14. There are altogether 45 ping pong balls in the three boxes A, B and C.

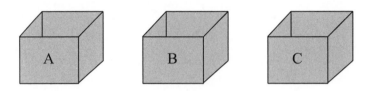

    7 ping pong balls are first transferred from box A to box B. 3 ping pong balls are then transferred from box B to box C. Finally, 6 ping pong balls are transferred from box C to box A. There are then equal number of ping pong balls in each box. Find the number of ping pong balls in each box at first.

15. This year Clarice is 9 years old and her sister is 21 years old. How many years ago was Clarice's sister three times her age?
    (*Hint:* The difference between two persons' age is always the same.
             You may draw a model to help you solve the problem.)

Take the Challenge!

1. Roxanne and May share a sum of money equally. Roxanne's share is a multiple of $8 and May's share is a multiple of $12. What is the largest possible sum of money shared by them if it does not exceed $200?

2. Bill's age this year is a multiple of 5.
   Next year, his age will be a multiple of 7.
   How old will Bill be next year?

3. There were a total of 40 round-shaped and heart-shaped gift boxes. A shop assistant put 4 cookies into each gift box. She soon realized that she did not have sufficient cookies to put into all the gift boxes. So, she put 4 cookies in each round-shaped gift box and only 3 cookies in each heart-shaped gift box. The total number of cookies in the round-shaped gift boxes was double the total number of cookies in the heart-shaped gift boxes. What was the total number of cookies?

Topic 2: Multiplication and Division of Whole Numbers

1. Multiply the following.

    (a) $\begin{array}{r} 1\ 8\ 3 \\ \times \qquad 8 \\ \hline \\ \hline \end{array}$

    (b) $\begin{array}{r} 4\ 8\ 7 \\ \times \qquad 4 \\ \hline \\ \hline \end{array}$

    (c) $\begin{array}{r} 3\ 7\ 9 \\ \times \qquad 6 \\ \hline \\ \hline \end{array}$

    (d) $\begin{array}{r} 1\ 0\ 7\ 8 \\ \times \qquad 9 \\ \hline \\ \hline \end{array}$

    (e) $\begin{array}{r} 3\ 7\ 1\ 9 \\ \times \qquad 3 \\ \hline \\ \hline \end{array}$

    (f) $\begin{array}{r} 2\ 9\ 0\ 4 \\ \times \qquad 8 \\ \hline \\ \hline \end{array}$

    (g) $\begin{array}{r} 4\ 2\ 0\ 9 \\ \times \qquad 5 \\ \hline \\ \hline \end{array}$

    (h) $\begin{array}{r} 8\ 4\ 5\ 3 \\ \times \qquad 6 \\ \hline \\ \hline \end{array}$

    (i) $\begin{array}{r} 9\ 8\ 7\ 0 \\ \times \qquad 7 \\ \hline \\ \hline \end{array}$

2. Estimate the product of the numbers in Question 1.

    (a) $183 \times 8 \approx 200 \times 8$
         $= 1600$

    (b) $487 \times 4 \approx$

    (c) $379 \times 6 \approx$

    (d) $1078 \times 9 \approx$

    (e) $3719 \times 3 \approx$

    (f) $2904 \times 8 \approx$

    (g) $4209 \times 5 \approx$

18

(h) $8453 \times 6 \approx$ (i) $9870 \times 7 \approx$

(j) What do you notice about the actual values and the corresponding estimated values in each question? What is the use of estimation?

_____

_____

3. Divide the following.

(a) $7 \overline{)\ 9\,9\,4}$ (b) $5 \overline{)\ 5\,0\,5}$

(c) $4 \overline{)\ 2\,2\,7\,6}$ (d) $7 \overline{)\ 4\,7\,4\,6}$

(e) $8 \overline{)\ 1\,7\,4\,4}$ (f) $9 \overline{)\ 2\,7\,3\,6}$

(g) $6 \overline{)\ 3\,6\,4\,8}$ (h) $8 \overline{)\ 7\,8\,9\,6}$

4. Estimate the quotient of the numbers in Question 3.

(a) $994 \div 7 \approx 980 \div 7$ (b) $505 \div 5 \approx$
              $= 140$

(c) $2276 \div 4 \approx$ (d) $4746 \div 7 \approx$

(e) $1744 \div 8 \approx$ (f) $2736 \div 9 \approx$

(g) $3648 \div 6 \approx$ (h) $7896 \div 8 \approx$

5. Divide the following.

(a) 70 ÷ 10 =

(b) 680 ÷ 10 =

(c) 900 ÷ 10 =

(d) 1240 ÷ 10 =

(e) 6030 ÷ 10 =

(f) 8000 ÷ 10 =

(g) 4629 ÷ 10 =

(h) 7027 ÷ 10 =

(i) 5247 ÷ 10 =

(j) 6956 ÷ 10 =

6. Multiply the following.

Example: $73 \times 40 = \boxed{73 \times 4} \times 10$
$$= 292 \times 10$$
$$= 2920$$

(a) 37 × 10 =

(b) 73 × 10 =

(c) 89 × 10 =

(d) 30 × 47 =

(e) 40 × 60 =

(f) 80 × 70 =

(g) 248 × 20 =

(h) 832 × 90 =

(i) 790 × 40 =

(j) 460 × 80 =

7. Multiply the following.

(a)
```
      4 9
×     2 6
_____


_____

_____
```

(b)
```
      8 7
×     4 3
_____


_____

_____
```

(c)
```
        3 8
  ×     6 2
  ─────────

  ─────────
```

(d)
```
        1 5
  ×     4 9
  ─────────

  ─────────
```

(e)
```
      2 3 8
  ×     5 4
  ─────────

  ─────────
```

(f)
```
      3 0 8
  ×     1 9
  ─────────

  ─────────
```

(g)
```
      7 0 6
  ×     3 6
  ─────────

  ─────────
```

(h)
```
      9 7 8
  ×     8 5
  ─────────

  ─────────
```

8. Estimate the product of the numbers in Question 7.

(a) $49 \times 26 \approx 50 \times 30$
              $= 1500$

(b) $87 \times 43 \approx$

(c) $38 \times 62 \approx$

(d) $15 \times 49 \approx$

(e) $238 \times 54 \approx$

(f) $308 \times 19 \approx$

(g) $706 \times 36 \approx$

(h) $978 \times 85 \approx$

9. Multiply these numbers.

Example: $36 \times 74 = 36 \times (70 + 4)$
$$= (36 \times 70) + (36 \times 4)$$
$$= 2520 + 144$$
$$= 2664$$

Note: $\square \times (\bigcirc + \triangle) = (\square \times \bigcirc) + (\square \times \triangle)$

(a) $43 \times 76 = 43 \times (70 + 6)$
$$=$$
$$=$$
$$=$$

(b) $68 \times 803 =$

(c) $95 \times 44 =$

(d) $405 \times 89 =$

10. Multiply these numbers.

Example: $39 \times 15 = (40 - 1) \times 15$
$$= (40 \times 15) - (1 \times 15)$$
$$= 600 - 15$$
$$= 585$$

Note: $(\bigcirc - \triangle) \times \square = (\bigcirc \times \square) - (\triangle \times \square)$

(a) $59 \times 32 = (60 - 1) \times 32$
$$=$$
$$=$$
$$=$$

(b) $67 \times 232 =$

(c) $46 \times 64 =$

(d) $701 \times 99 =$

11. Fill in the missing number in each box.
You may use the methods learned in Questions 9 and 10.

(a) $78 \times 23 = 23 \times 70 + \boxed{}$

(b) $418 \times 99 = 100 \times 418 - \boxed{}$

(c) $200 \times 33 - \boxed{} = 198 \times 33$

(d) $128 \times 100 + \boxed{} = 102 \times 128$

12. Multiply using factors.
Fill in the missing number in each box.

Example: $132 \times 25 = 660 \times 5$

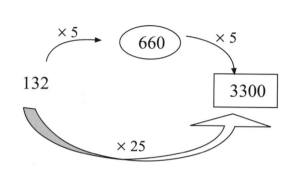

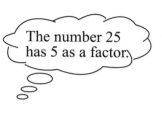

The number 25 has 5 as a factor.

(a) $48 \times 125 = \boxed{} \times 25$

(b) $32 \times \boxed{} = 25 \times 256$

(c) $49 \times \boxed{} = 98 \times 25$

(d) $150 \times 207 = 621 \times \boxed{}$

(e) If $7 \times 144 = 1008$, then $21 \times 144 = \boxed{}$

(f) Given $35 \times 13 = 455$, then $35 \times 39 = \boxed{}$

(g) Given $27 \times 136 = 3672$, then $108 \times 136 = \boxed{}$

13. Use the models to complete the solution to each of the following questions.

(a) Ali, Bernard and Charles collected a total of $5562 for their school sports fund. Bernard collected twice as much as Ali. Charles collected three times as much as Bernard. How much more did Charles collect than Bernard?

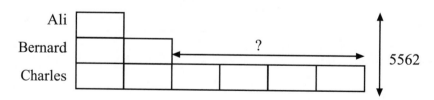

1 unit = 5562 ÷ 9 = $618

Charles → 618 × _____ = _____

Charles collected $_____ more.

24

(b) Both Tara and Will earned the same salary. Tara spent $1809 and Will spent $42. Then Will had 4 times the amount of money Tara had left. How much is their salary?

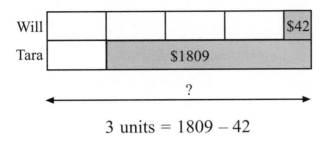

$$3 \text{ units} = 1809 - 42$$

(c) Daryl has 23 more picture cards than Edward. Gerald has twice the total number of picture cards Daryl and Edward have. Altogether the three boys have 1803 picture cards. How many more picture cards does Gerald have than Edward has?

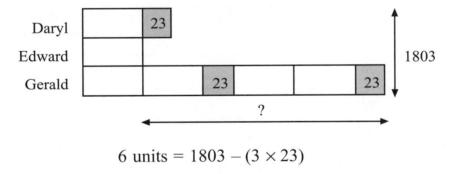

$$6 \text{ units} = 1803 - (3 \times 23)$$

WORD PROBLEMS

1. The number of cars is 5 times the number of vans in a business district. There are 3576 vehicles in all.
   (a) How many vans are there?
   (b) How many more cars than vans are there?

2. Nathan spends $1743 of his monthly salary and saves the remaining $435. What is his total salary for half a year?

3. Mr. Mustafa made 8396 curry puffs in his factory on a certain day. He delivered 268 curry puffs to a customer. He packed the rest of the curry puffs in boxes of 8 for sale in shops. How many boxes did he use to pack them?

4. The table below shows the number of story books read by some boys in a class.

Number of boys	Number of story books read by each boy
1	34
5	20
10	15
14	10

What is the total number of books read?

5. A machine can produce 5504 meatballs in 8 hours. How many meatballs can the machine produce in a day if it runs continuously for 24 hours?

6. A fruit grocer bought 18 baskets of grapefruits. Each basket contained 45 grapefruits. He threw away 6 bad grapefruits from each basket and sold the rest. How many grapefruits did he sell?

7. Mr. Ping took a car loan from a bank. He repaid the bank in monthly installments of $963 for a period of 7 years. If he paid a total interest of $12,892 during the period, what was the amount of the car loan? (Note: Interest was paid in the monthly installments.)

8. On an Australian farm, there were 205 ostriches. Each ostrich laid 3 eggs on a particular day. If the farmer sold each ostrich egg for 80 cents, how much money did he earn for that day?

9. Mrs. Dawson saved $2192 in two years. She saved $88 every month for the first 14 months. She saved an equal amount of money for the remaining months. How much did she save in each of the remaining months?

10. The cost of tickets for a circus performance is as follows:

   Adult — $7

   Child — $3

On a Sunday, the total sale of tickets was $12,680.
Each parent brought one child to the circus.
How many people watched the circus performance that day?

11. Patsy has 78 fewer stamps than Sam.
Britney has 59 more stamps than the total number of stamps Patsy and Sam have. If Britney has 253 more stamps than Patsy, how many stamps does Britney have?

12. Erin and Josie collected 5488 coins from all over the world. If Erin gave 1407 of her coins to Josie, Josie would have 6 times as many coins as Erin. How many coins did each girl collect?

13. There were three times as many jelly beans in Jar A as in Jar B. After 2685 jelly beans in Jar A were sold, Jar B had twice as many jelly beans as Jar A. How many more jelly beans were there in Jar A than in Jar B at first?

14. Aileen and Barry had an equal number of postcards. After Barry had given Aileen 20 postcards, Aileen had five times as many postcards as Barry. Find their total number of postcards.

15. (a) Peter had a total of 36 quarters and dimes. If he had $6 in all, how many quarters did he have?
    (*Hint:* Use Guess and Check method.)
    (b) A lady bought 6 packets of white buttons and 3 packets of black buttons. There were altogether 120 buttons. Each packet of black buttons contained three times as many buttons as each packet of white buttons. How many white buttons did she buy?

-Take the Challenge!

1. On one side of a straight long road, there are many street lights, equidistant from one another. The distance between the 1st street light and the 5th street light is 200 yards. Find the distance between the 1st street light and the 20th street light.
   (*Hint:* Draw a picture to help you figure out the answer.)

2. A baker made some muffins yesterday. He needed to put them all into round boxes that came in two sizes. A small box can hold 7 muffins while a big box can hold 13 muffins. There were at total of 106 muffins. How many small boxes and big boxes did the baker use?

3. A machine processing pizzas in a factory puts the following ingredients on top of pizzas in this order,

> Canadian bacon to every 8th pizza,
> pieces of pineapple to every 9th pizza,
> green peppers to every 12th pizza.

Since it was switched on at the beginning of the week, the machine has processed 100,000 pizzas.

(a) How many of the pizzas have all the three toppings of Canadian bacon, pineapple pieces and green peppers?

(b) How many of the pizzas have toppings of Canadian bacon and green peppers without pineapple pieces?

4.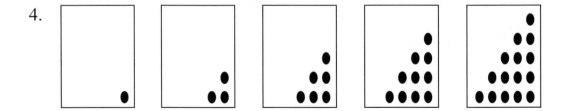

Study the dot pattern in the cards above carefully.
What is the number of dots to be drawn on the 10th card?

Topic 3: Fractions

1. Divide each bar into equal parts and shade the fraction indicated.

(a)

1 whole

$\dfrac{2}{3}$

(b)

$\dfrac{5}{8}$

(c)

$\dfrac{5}{6}$

(d)

$\dfrac{3}{7}$

(e) The fraction above that shows the largest part of the whole is

_____.

(f) The fraction above that shows the smallest part of the whole is

_____.

2. Divide each bar into equal parts to find the missing number in each box.

(a) $\dfrac{1}{2} = \dfrac{\square}{6}$

(b) $\dfrac{1}{5} = \dfrac{\square}{10}$

(c) $\dfrac{2}{3} = \dfrac{\square}{9}$

(d) $\dfrac{3}{4} = \dfrac{\square}{8}$

31

3. Fill in the missing numbers in the boxes.

(a) $\dfrac{1}{2} = \dfrac{\Box}{8} = \dfrac{\Box}{4}$

(b) $\dfrac{1}{3} = \dfrac{\Box}{6} = \dfrac{\Box}{9}$

(c) $\dfrac{5}{6} = \dfrac{10}{\Box} = \dfrac{\Box}{18}$

(d) $\dfrac{\Box}{3} = \dfrac{8}{12} = \dfrac{\Box}{6}$

4. Express the following fractions in their simplest forms.

(a) $\dfrac{4}{10} =$

(b) $\dfrac{3}{12} =$

(c) $\dfrac{6}{8} =$

(d) $\dfrac{12}{15} =$

(e) $\dfrac{6}{21} =$

(f) $\dfrac{6}{9} =$

5. Arrange the fractions in ascending order.

(a) $\dfrac{1}{2}, \dfrac{1}{3}, \dfrac{1}{12}, \dfrac{1}{8}$ _____

(b) $\dfrac{12}{15}, \dfrac{4}{15}, \dfrac{7}{15}, \dfrac{2}{15}$ _____

(c) $\dfrac{5}{8}, \dfrac{1}{3}, \dfrac{3}{4}, 1$ _____

(d) $\dfrac{3}{4}, \dfrac{2}{3}, \dfrac{11}{12}, \dfrac{1}{5}$ _____

6. Arrange the fractions in descending order.

(a) $\dfrac{1}{6}, \dfrac{1}{2}, \dfrac{1}{5}, \dfrac{1}{9}$ _____

(b) $\dfrac{2}{13}, \dfrac{7}{13}, \dfrac{4}{13}, \dfrac{11}{13}$ _____

(c) $\dfrac{1}{8}, \dfrac{2}{10}, \dfrac{3}{4}, \dfrac{11}{12}$ _____

(d) $\dfrac{3}{8}, \dfrac{2}{3}, \dfrac{11}{12}, \dfrac{1}{4}$ _____

7. Add and give each answer in its simplest form.

(a) $\dfrac{1}{4} + \dfrac{2}{4} =$

(b) $\dfrac{3}{5} + \dfrac{1}{5} =$

(c) $\dfrac{3}{8} + \dfrac{2}{8} =$

(d) $\dfrac{4}{7} + \dfrac{3}{7} =$

(e) $\dfrac{2}{9} + \dfrac{4}{9} =$

(f) $\dfrac{11}{15} + \dfrac{2}{15} =$

(g) $\dfrac{3}{12} + \dfrac{5}{12} + \dfrac{2}{12} =$

(h) $\dfrac{4}{14} + \dfrac{3}{14} + \dfrac{5}{14} =$

(i) $\dfrac{3}{10} + \dfrac{1}{10} + \dfrac{2}{10} =$

(j) $\dfrac{2}{6} + \dfrac{3}{6} + \dfrac{1}{6} =$

8. Subtract and give each answer in its simplest form.

(a) $\dfrac{7}{9} - \dfrac{2}{9} =$

(b) $\dfrac{4}{5} - \dfrac{2}{5} =$

(c) $\dfrac{4}{6} - \dfrac{1}{6} =$

(d) $1 - \dfrac{6}{10} =$

(e) $1 - \dfrac{8}{12} =$

(f) $1 - \dfrac{3}{4} =$

(g) $\dfrac{7}{8} - \dfrac{3}{8} =$

(h) $1 - \dfrac{3}{14} - \dfrac{5}{14} =$

(i) $\dfrac{9}{11} - \dfrac{3}{11} - \dfrac{4}{11} =$

(j) $1 - \dfrac{1}{3} - \dfrac{2}{3} =$

9. Add and give each answer in its simplest form.

(a) $\dfrac{1}{4} + \dfrac{1}{2} =$

(b) $\dfrac{2}{9} + \dfrac{2}{3} =$

(c) $\dfrac{2}{3} + \dfrac{3}{12} =$

(d) $\dfrac{2}{6} + \dfrac{1}{3} =$

(e) $\dfrac{2}{5} + \dfrac{3}{10} =$

(f) $\dfrac{3}{12} + \dfrac{1}{4} =$

(g) $\dfrac{1}{3} + \dfrac{2}{9} + \dfrac{4}{9} =$

(h) $\dfrac{1}{8} + \dfrac{1}{4} + \dfrac{1}{2} =$

(i) $\dfrac{3}{10} + \dfrac{1}{5} + \dfrac{3}{10} =$

(j) $\dfrac{1}{6} + \dfrac{1}{12} + \dfrac{5}{12} =$

10. Subtract and give each answer in its simplest form.

(a) $\dfrac{1}{2} - \dfrac{1}{4} =$

(b) $\dfrac{7}{9} - \dfrac{2}{3} =$

(c) $\dfrac{4}{5} - \dfrac{3}{10} =$

(d) $\dfrac{1}{2} - \dfrac{4}{10} =$

(e) $\dfrac{3}{4} - \dfrac{3}{12} =$

(f) $\dfrac{7}{10} - \dfrac{1}{2} =$

(g) $1 - \dfrac{3}{8} - \dfrac{1}{4} =$

(h) $1 - \dfrac{1}{3} - \dfrac{4}{9} =$

(i) $1 - \dfrac{1}{5} - \dfrac{7}{10} =$

(j) $\dfrac{5}{6} - \dfrac{1}{12} - \dfrac{1}{6} =$

11. Answer the following questions. Give each answer in its simplest form.

(a) Valerie spent $\dfrac{3}{8}$ of her pocket money and saved the rest. What fraction of her pocket money did she save?

(b) Mr. Jones drank $\dfrac{1}{5}$ of the milk in a carton. His children drank $\dfrac{3}{10}$ of it. What fraction of the milk in the carton did they drink altogether?

(c) Aaron used $\dfrac{2}{3}$ gallon of paint to paint a door and $\dfrac{1}{6}$ gallon of paint to paint a book shelf. How much more paint did he use to paint the door than the book shelf?

(d) Pat baked a pizza. She ate $\frac{1}{3}$ of the pizza and her brother ate $\frac{5}{12}$ of it. What fraction of the pizza was left?

(e) Paula bought $\frac{2}{5}$ lb of apples and $\frac{1}{10}$ lb more grapes. How many pounds of fruits did she buy altogether?

(f) There are some marbles in a box. $\frac{1}{6}$ of the marbles are yellow, $\frac{1}{4}$ of them are blue and the rest are red marbles. What fraction of the marbles in the box are red?

12. Look at the diagrams and fill in the blanks.

(a)

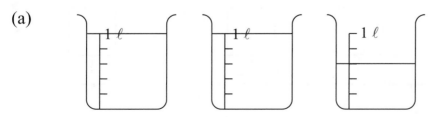

The total amount of water in the three beakers is _____ ℓ.

(b)

The grapes weigh _____ lb.

(c)

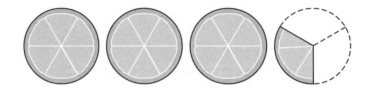

There are _____ pizzas.

(d)

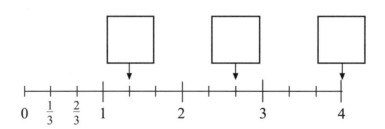

(e)

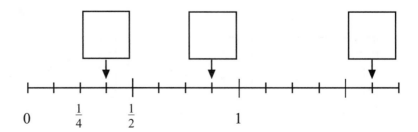

36

13. Write each answer as a mixed number.

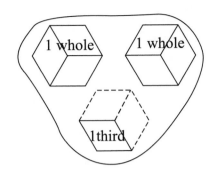 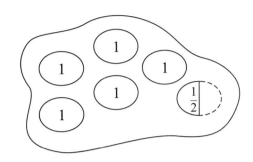

(a) $2 + \dfrac{1}{3} =$

(b) $4 + \dfrac{2}{5} =$

(c) $\dfrac{1}{4} + 9 =$

(d) $\dfrac{7}{12} + 3 =$

(e) $6 - \dfrac{1}{2} =$

(f) $7 - \dfrac{3}{7} =$

(g) $12 - \dfrac{3}{4} =$

(h) $10 - \dfrac{1}{5} =$

14. Write each of the following as an improper fraction in its simplest form.

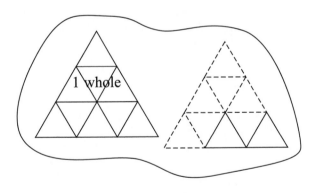 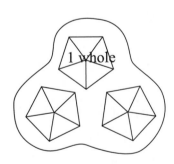

(a) 6 quarters =

(b) 7 halves =

(c) 5 thirds =

(d) 15 fifths =

(e) 8 sixths =

(f) 9 eighths =

(g) 1 whole 2 ninths =

(h) 5 wholes 2 thirds =

(i) 3 wholes 3 quarters =

(j) 6 wholes 5 sevenths =

15. Express each mixed number as an improper fraction.

(a) $1\frac{4}{7} = \frac{7}{7} + \frac{4}{7}$

$= $

(b) $2\frac{1}{3} = \frac{\boxed{}}{3} + \frac{1}{3}$

$= $

(c) $5\frac{2}{5} = $

(d) $4\frac{1}{2} = $

(e) $3\frac{2}{9} = $

(f) $2\frac{3}{4} = $

(g) $2\frac{3}{10} = $

(h) $1\frac{7}{12} = $

16. Express each of the following as a whole number or a mixed number in its simplest form.

(a) $\frac{17}{6} = \frac{12}{6} + \frac{5}{6}$

$= $

(b) $\frac{12}{5} = \frac{10}{5} + \frac{\boxed{}}{5}$

$= $

(c) $\frac{18}{3} = $

(d) $\frac{11}{4} = $

(e) $\frac{12}{9} = $

(f) $\frac{21}{7} = $

(g) $1\frac{7}{5} = $

(h) $3\frac{8}{4} = $

(i) $4\frac{11}{6} = $

(j) $2\frac{16}{10} = $

17. Add and give each answer as a fraction or a mixed number in its simplest form.

(a) $\frac{2}{4} + \frac{3}{4} = $

(b) $\frac{4}{5} + \frac{3}{5} = $

(c) $\frac{7}{9} + \frac{1}{3} = $

(d) $\frac{5}{6} + \frac{2}{3} = $

(e) $\dfrac{11}{12} + \dfrac{5}{6} =$

(f) $\dfrac{1}{4} + \dfrac{1}{3} =$

(g) $\dfrac{3}{10} + \dfrac{2}{5} + \dfrac{3}{5} =$

(h) $\dfrac{1}{3} + \dfrac{5}{6} + 1 =$

18. Subtract and give each answer as a fraction or a mixed number in its simplest form.

(a) $1 - \dfrac{4}{9} =$

(b) $2 - \dfrac{4}{5} =$

(c) $\dfrac{1}{2} - \dfrac{3}{10} =$

(d) $\dfrac{5}{8} - \dfrac{1}{4} =$

(e) $\dfrac{7}{12} - \dfrac{1}{4} =$

(f) $\dfrac{1}{2} - \dfrac{1}{5} =$

(g) $1\dfrac{3}{4} - \dfrac{3}{8} =$

(h) $2\dfrac{9}{10} - \dfrac{1}{2} =$

19. Fill in the blanks.

(a) There are _____ halves $\left(\dfrac{1}{2}\right)$ in $\dfrac{6}{2}$.

(b) There are _____ halves $\left(\dfrac{1}{2}\right)$ in $5\dfrac{1}{2}$.

(c) There are _____ thirds $\left(\dfrac{1}{3}\right)$ in $2\dfrac{2}{3}$.

(d) There are _____ thirds $\left(\dfrac{1}{3}\right)$ in $1\dfrac{3}{9}$.

(e) There are _____ quarters $\left(\dfrac{1}{4}\right)$ in $4\dfrac{1}{2}$.

(f) There are _____ quarters $\left(\dfrac{1}{4}\right)$ in 3 wholes.

(g) There are _____ sixths $\left(\dfrac{1}{6}\right)$ in $\dfrac{2}{3}$.

(h) There are _____ eighths $\left(\dfrac{1}{8}\right)$ in $3\dfrac{3}{4}$.

(i) There are _____ tenths $\left(\dfrac{1}{10}\right)$ in $3\dfrac{1}{5}$.

20. Write 'smaller than', 'equal to' or 'greater than' in each box.

(a) $1\frac{1}{4}$ is [ ] $\frac{5}{6}$

(b) $\frac{4}{5}$ is [ ] $2\frac{1}{3}$

(c) $\frac{8}{9}$ is [ ] $\frac{7}{5}$

(d) $\frac{10}{4}$ is [ ] $2\frac{1}{4}$

(e) $1\frac{4}{9}$ is [ ] $\frac{13}{9}$

(f) $2\frac{9}{10}$ is [ ] $\frac{7}{3}$

(g) $3\frac{1}{3}$ is [ ] $\frac{20}{6}$

(h) $\frac{9}{7}$ is [ ] $\frac{13}{6}$

21. What fraction of the whole is each of the following?
Fill in each blank with the correct fraction in its simplest form.

(a)

Out of every 6 beads,
3 of them are ◇-shaped.

_____ of the string of beads
are ◇-shaped.

40

(b)

For every 8 beads in this string, 5 of them are ⬭-shaped.

_____ of the string of beads are ⬭-shaped.

(c)

There are 6 tables and chairs.

The chairs make up _____ of the six items.

(d)

There are a total of 7 chairs and tables.

_____ of the seven items are tables.

22. In each of the following, express the shaded part as a fraction of the figure in its simplest form.

(a)

_____

(b)

_____

(c)

_____

(d)

_____

(e)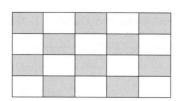

(f)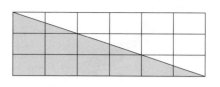

_____ _____

(g)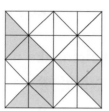

(h)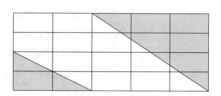

_____ _____

23. Shade each figure in the right column in a different way to show the **same fraction** as shown in the figure in the left column. Write the fraction in the box.

(a)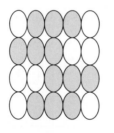

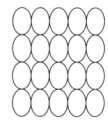

(b)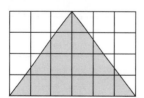

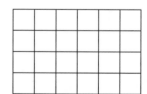

(c)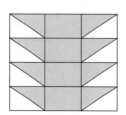

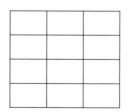

42

(d)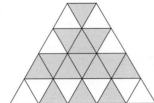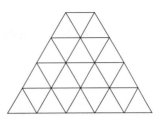

24. Find the value represented by a fraction of a set.

Example: There are 12 eggs in an egg carton.

I use $\frac{1}{3}$ of the eggs to make an omelette.

What does this mean? How many eggs have I used?

12 eggs

?		

3 thirds ⟶ 12 eggs

1 third ⟶ $\frac{1}{3}$ of 12

= 12 ÷ 3 = 4 eggs

(a) $\frac{2}{3}$ of 27 boys = $\frac{2}{3}$ × 27

= _____ boys

(b) $\frac{3}{8}$ of 32 chairs = $\frac{3}{8}$ × 32

= _____ chairs

(c) $\frac{4}{5}$ of 20 coins =

= _____ coins

(d) $\frac{3}{4}$ of 16 stamps =

= _____ stamps

(e) $\frac{1}{6}$ of 36 marbles   =

         = _____ marbles

(f) $\frac{5}{7}$ of 21 CDs =

         = _____ CDs

(g)   What do you notice about the values represented by their fractions?
      Can the result be a fraction?

      _____

25.   Find the value represented by a fraction of a set.
      Give the answer as a whole number or a fraction in its simplest form.

Example: $\frac{2}{3}$ of 8 apples

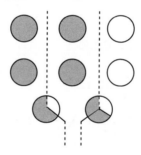

$$\frac{2}{3} \times 8 = \frac{16}{3} = 5\frac{1}{3} \text{ apples}$$

(a) $\frac{7}{8}$ of 20 km =

         = _____ km

(b) $\frac{3}{5}$ of 8 qt   =

         = _____ qt

(c) $\frac{1}{4}$ of 23 in. =

         = _____ in.

44

(d) $\dfrac{5}{6}$ of 15 pizzas =

= _____ pizzas

(e) $\dfrac{2}{3}$ of 7 hours =

= _____ hours

(f) $\dfrac{2}{9}$ of $45 =

= $ _____

26. Write each of the following as a fraction in its simplest form.

(a) What fraction of 1 year is 5 months?

(b) Express 750 g as a fraction of 1 kg.

(c) Express 25 minutes as a fraction of $1\dfrac{1}{2}$ hours.

(d) What fraction of 1 liter of milk is 800 ml of milk?

(e) Eunice bought a bouquet of 32 roses for her mother on her birthday. 20 were pink roses. What fraction of the bouquet were pink roses?

(f) Mrs. Penny sold a total of 35 blue and red pens. 10 of them were red pens. What fraction of the pens sold were blue pens?

(g) Clarissa spent $36 of her savings on a Barbie doll. What fraction of her savings did she spend if she had saved $60?

(h) There are 84 story books in a class library. Students borrowed 60 story books. What fraction of the story books were left in the class library?

27. In each of the following squares, the value of the shaded part is given. Find the value(s) of the other part(s) as indicated and the value of the whole square. Fill in the boxes and blanks accordingly.

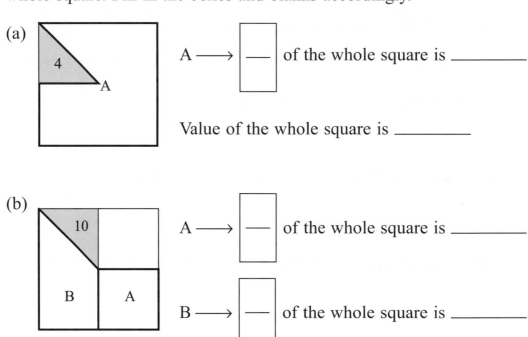

(a)

A ⟶ $\boxed{}$ of the whole square is _____

Value of the whole square is _____

(b)

A ⟶ $\boxed{}$ of the whole square is _____

B ⟶ $\boxed{}$ of the whole square is _____

Value of the whole square is _____

(c)

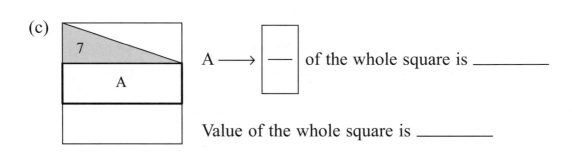

A ⟶ $\boxed{}$ of the whole square is _____

Value of the whole square is _____

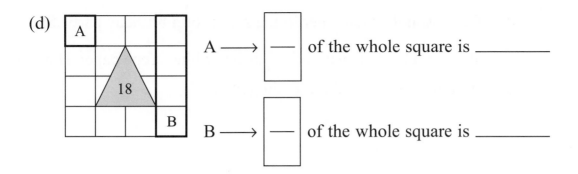

(d)

A $\longrightarrow$ $\boxed{}$ of the whole square is _____

B $\longrightarrow$ $\boxed{}$ of the whole square is _____

Value of the whole square is _____

WORD PROBLEMS

1. Tom had a full tank of gas in his car. His car consumed $\frac{2}{9}$ of the tank of gas on Saturday and $\frac{1}{3}$ of it on Sunday. What fraction of the tank of gas was left after the weekend?

2. The sum of $\frac{1}{3}$ and $\frac{1}{2}$ is half of the fraction I am thinking of. What is the fraction? Give the answer as an improper fraction, in its simplest form.

3. Mrs. Thompson decorated her living room for a birthday party. She used $2\frac{1}{2}$ rolls of red crepe paper and $3\frac{1}{3}$ rolls of blue crepe paper. How many rolls of crepe paper did she use altogether?

4. The Lim family spent $5\frac{5}{8}$ hours on Saturday and $3\frac{3}{8}$ hours on Sunday painting the rooms in their house. How many more hours did they work on Saturday than on Sunday?

5. Mrs. Shanti bought 1 lb of flour. She used $\frac{1}{2}$ lb of flour on Monday and $\frac{3}{8}$ lb on Tuesday. How much flour did she have left?

6. Shawn collected 24 stamps. 16 of them were local stamps and the rest were foreign stamps. What fraction of Shawn's stamps were foreign stamps? Give the answer in its simplest form.

7. A kitten weighs $\frac{5}{6}$ kg. A puppy weighs $\frac{2}{3}$ kg more than a kitten. How much do both the kitten and the puppy weigh? Give the answer in its simplest form.

8. Chris ran $\frac{7}{8}$ mi along a jogging track. His friend ran $\frac{1}{4}$ mi less far than he ran. What was the total distance they ran? Give the answer in its simplest form.

9. Cherry saved some money last month. She used $\frac{3}{8}$ of her savings to buy a toy. The toy cost $27. How much did Cherry save last month?

10. Mrs. Weatherby baked 175 cookies for a party. The children ate $\frac{4}{7}$ of the cookies. The adults ate 48 cookies. How many cookies were left?

11. Jared has some marbles. $\frac{3}{5}$ of the marbles are red, $\frac{1}{10}$ of them are green and the rest are blue. If Jared has 30 blue marbles, how many marbles does he have altogether?

12. (a) In the figure, 4 small squares are shaded. How many more small squares must be shaded so that $\frac{2}{5}$ of the figure gets shaded?

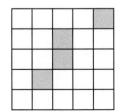

(b) A piece of rope 2 meters long is cut into 12 equal parts. What is the total length of 2 such parts? Give the answer as a fraction in its simplest form.

13. (a) Look at the number line below.

X is a mixed number. What number does it represent?

(b) Mrs. Bong bought 5 lb of rice. After a week, she found that she had used up $\frac{7}{10}$ of the rice. How much rice did she use in the week? Give the answer in pounds.

14. A bakery sold 45 buns on the first day. It sold $\frac{4}{5}$ as many buns on the second day.
    (a) How many buns were sold on the second day?
    (b) Express the number of buns sold on the second day as a fraction of the total number of buns sold in the two days. Give the answer in its simplest form.

15. Yasmine has 48 crystal stones. One-sixth of the crystal stones are red, one-quarter of the remaining crystal stones are blue and the rest are green.
    (a) How many green crystal stones does Yasmine have?
    (b) What fraction of the total number of crystal stones are green? (Give the answer in its simplest form.)

Take the Challenge!

1. Mrs. Simon bought some lemons from the supermarket. She used $\frac{1}{3}$ of the lemons to make lemonade. She then gave 10 lemons to her neighbor. After that she still had 14 lemons left. How many lemons did Mrs. Simon buy?

2. A grocer sold a carton of apples to some customers. The first customer tasted one apple and bought half of the remaining apples. The second and third customers did the same. The fourth customer also tasted one apple and bought the remaining 23 apples. How many apples were there in the carton at first?

3. You fell ill and consulted a doctor. Your doctor gave you ten pills and told you to take one every half an hour. How many hours would the pills last?

4. A goldsmith has a big cube made of gold. It weighs 40 kg. He has a smaller cube of gold which has sides $\frac{1}{2}$ as long as the side of the big cube. How heavy is the smaller cube of gold?

   (*Hint:* The length, width and height of a cube are equal.)

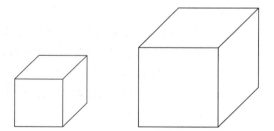

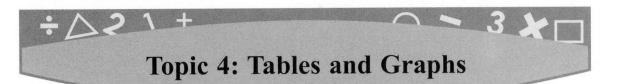

Topic 4: Tables and Graphs

1. The table shows the number of students in thee clubs in a particular school.

Uniform group	Number of students
Computer Club	150
Drama Club	100
Chess Club	120

Complete the graph below to represent the above data.

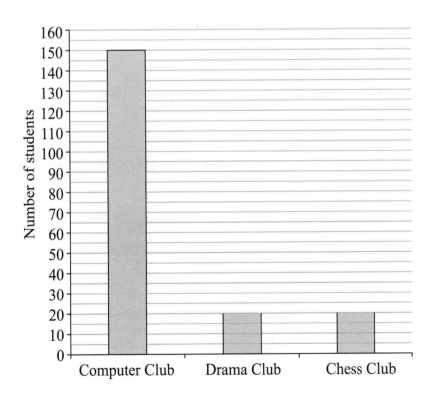

2. Mr. Tan sold the following number of fruits:

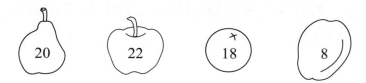

Complete the following graph to represent the above data.

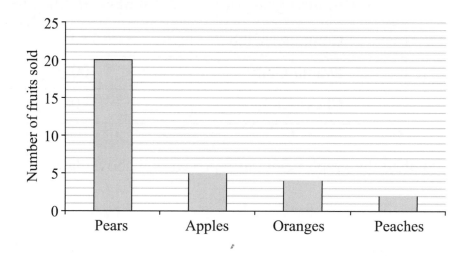

3. The table shows the number of books read by five fourth grade students since they were in second grade.

Name	Number of story books read
Jeremy	60
Paul	48
John	52
Sean	66
Gabriel	68

Complete the following graph to represent the given data.

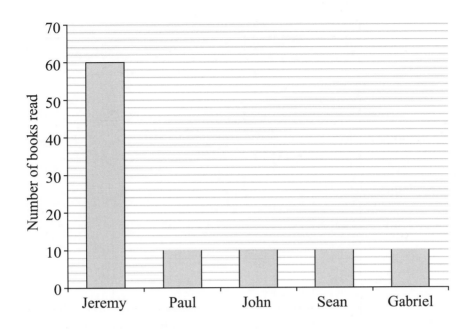

4. The table shows the number of cars sold by a car company in the second half of the year.

Month	Number of cars sold
July	200
August	360
September	450
October	320
November	500
December	660

Complete the following graph to represent the given data.

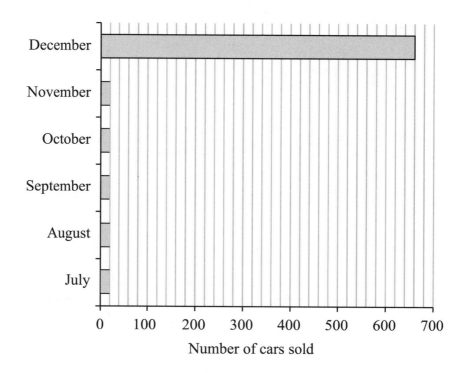

Number of cars sold

5. The table shows the number of grapefruits sold at a grocery store in a week.

Day	Number of grapefruits sold
Monday	60
Tuesday	50
Wednesday	40
Thursday	60
Friday	90
Saturday	105
Sunday	120

Complete the following graph to show the given data.

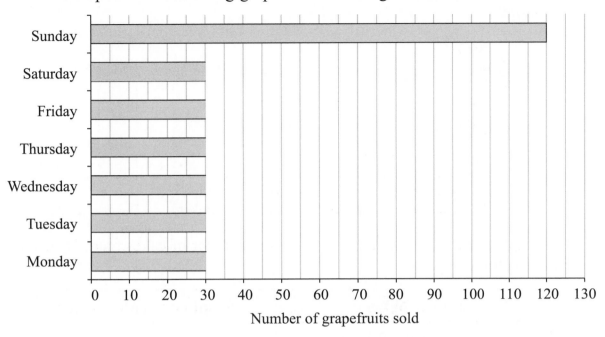

Number of grapefruits sold

6. The bar graph shows the number of pairs of shoes each child has.

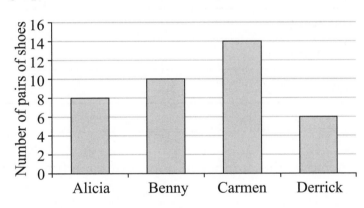

Complete the table below to show the data given in the graph.

Name	Number of pairs of shoes
Alicia	
Benny	
Carmen	
Derrick	

Total number of pairs of shoes = _____

7. The following bar graph shows the number of cakes each bakery made in a month.

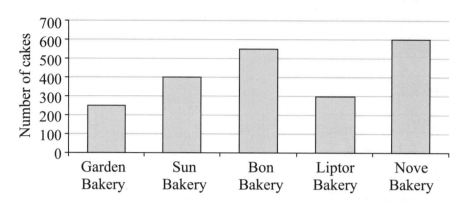

Complete the following table to show the number of cakes made by each bakery in a month.

Name of bakery	Number of cakes made
Garden Bakery	
Sun Bakery	
Bon Bakery	
Liptor Bakery	
Nove Bakery	

Total number of cakes made = _____

8. The bar graph shows the number of copies of each type of magazine sold in a month.

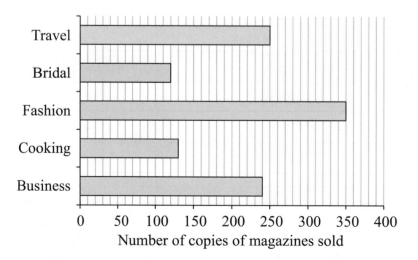

Complete the table below to show the number of each type of magazine sold.

Type of magazine	Number of copies of magazines sold
Business	
Cooking	
Fashion	
Bridal	
Travel	

Total number of copies of magazines sold = _____

9. The bar graph shows the points six students scored on their math final.

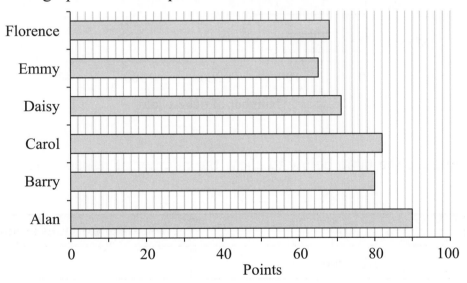

Complete the table below to show the points scored by the students.

Name	Points
Alan	
Barry	
Carol	
Daisy	
Emmy	
Florence	

Total number of points = _____

10. The bar graph shows the number of tickets sold each day of a particular week for a movie.

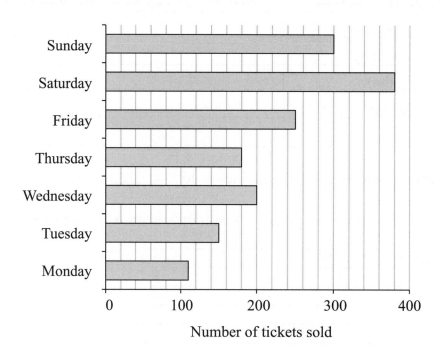

Number of tickets sold

Complete the table below to show the number of tickets sold.

Day	Number of tickets sold
Monday	
Tuesday	
Wednesday	
Thursday	
Friday	
Saturday	
Sunday	

Total number of tickets sold = _____

11. The bar graph shows the number of each type of compact discs (CDs) sold at a music store in a particular week.
Study the graph and answer the questions below.

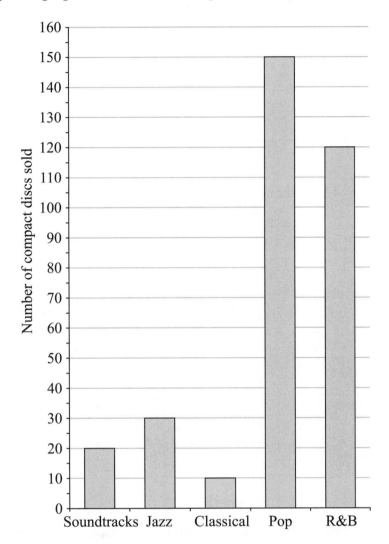

(a) Based on the sales for the week, which was the most popular type of music? _____

(b) How many R&B compact discs were sold in the week? _____

(c) How many more Jazz CDs than Soundtrack CDs were sold? _____

(d) If Classical CDs cost $20 each, how much was the total collection from the sale of the Classical CDs in the week? _____

(e) What was the total number of CDs sold in the week? _____

12. The bar graph shows the number of cookies a baker made in the years 1997 to 2001.
Study the graph and answer the questions that follow.

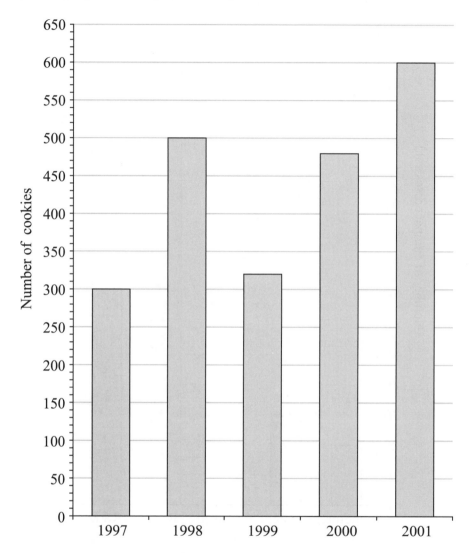

(a) How many more cookies did the baker make in 1998 than in 1999? _____

(b) How many cookies did she make in all? _____

(c) If she sold the cookies for 35 cents each in the years 1997 to 1999, how much did she receive from the sales? _____

(d) The baker increased the price of each cookie to 40 cents in the years 2000 and 2001. How much did she collect in these two years? _____

(e) How much did she collect in the 5 years? _____

13. The graph shows the number of students who have enrolled in the different subjects at a community college.
Study the graph and answer the questions that follow.

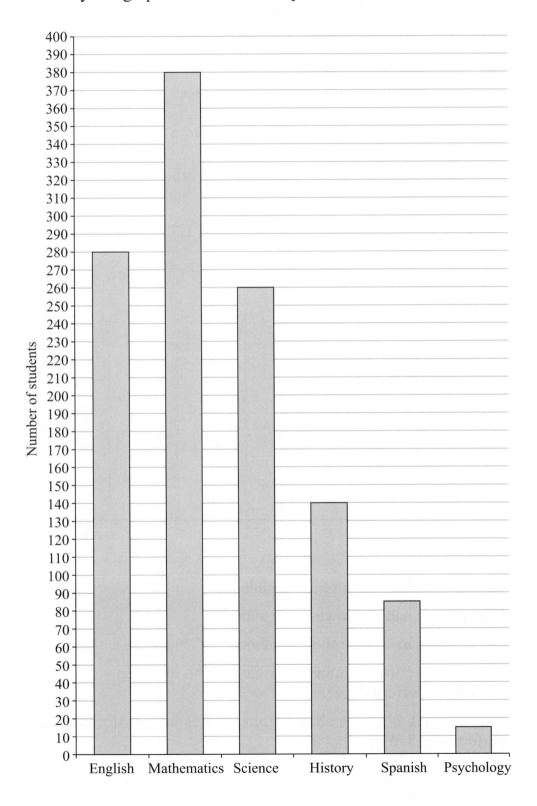

(a) Which subject has the highest enrollment? _____

(b) Which subject has an enrollment of 260 students? _____

(c) Which subject has twice the enrollment for history? _____

(d) What is the total enrollment for English, history, Spanish, and psychology? _____

(e) What is the total enrollment in the 6 classes? _____

14. The bar graph shows the number of students from different classes who attended a school performance.
Study the graph and answer the questions that follow.

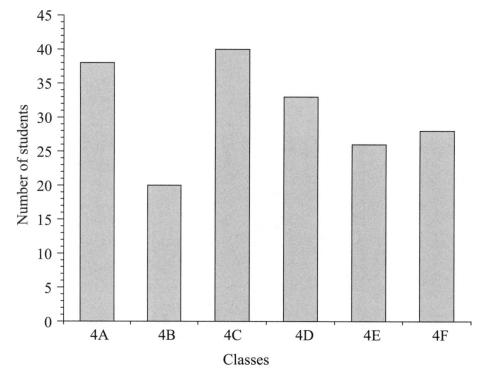

(a) Which class had the highest attendance? _____

(b) Which class had the lowest attendance? _____

(c) Which class had twice the attendance of Class 4B? _____

(d) What was the total number of students who attended the school performance? _____

(e) Do you think all the students from Classes 4A to 4F attended the performance? Why?

_____

15. The bar graph shows the amount of money Angela saved last week. Study the graph and answer the questions that follow.

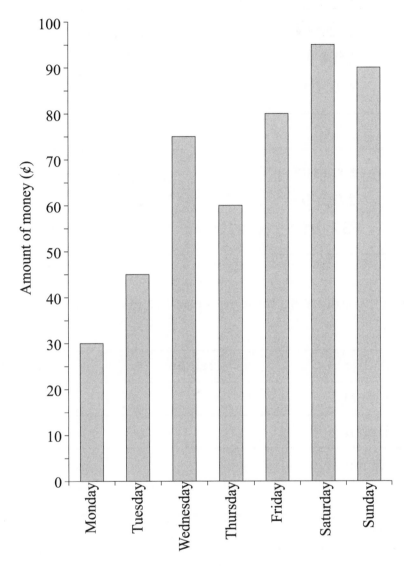

(a) On which day did Angela save 45 cents? _____

(b) How much did she save on Monday and Tuesday? _____

(c) On which day did she save the second highest amount of money? _____

(d) Angela used all the money she saved for the week to buy a birthday present for her mother. How much did the present cost? _____

(e) If Angela saved twice as much money this week than last week, how much did she save this week? _____

16. The weight and height of four boys are shown below.

Lionel	Bryan
Lionel 104 lb 60 in.	**Bryan** 120 lb 59 in.
Shaun 100 lb 62 in.	**Frank** 132 lb 68 in.

Complete the following table to show the given data.

Name	Height	Weight
Lionel		
Bryan		
Shaun		
Frank		
Total		

(a) Who is the heaviest boy? _____

(b) Who is the tallest boy? _____

(c) Who is taller but not as heavy as Lionel? _____

17. The prices of three different brands of orange juice are shown below.

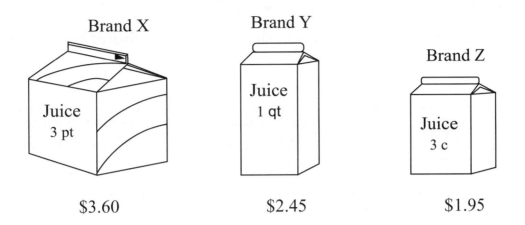

Brand X

Juice
3 pt

$3.60

Brand Y

Juice
1 qt

$2.45

Brand Z

Juice
3 c

$1.95

Complete the table below to show the given data.

Brand of juice	Capacity of carton	Price
X		
Y		
Z		

(a) Carol bought 3 cartons of Brand Y juice and
2 cartons of Brand Z juice. How much did she
pay for them? _____

(b) Carol gave $20 to the cashier at the supermarket.
How much change did she receive? _____

(c) Which is the most expensive brand of orange juice?_____

18. The table below shows the number of bowls of potato soup and clam chowder a restaurant sold last week. A bowl of potato soup costs $2.50 and a bowl of clam chowder costs $3.00.

Complete the following table to show the total number of bowls of potato soup and clam chowder sold.

Day	Number of bowls of potato soup	Number of bowls of clam chowder
Monday	20	25
Tuesday	24	31
Wednesday	36	25
Thursday	39	36
Friday	42	15
Saturday	66	36
Sunday	68	67
Total		

(a) On which day did the restaurant sell the most number of bowls of clam chowder? _____

(b) How many bowls of potato soup and clam chowder did the restaurant sell altogether? _____

(c) On which day did the restaurant make the most money from these two soups? _____

(d) How much did the restaurant collect on the day the least number of soup was sold? _____

19. The table below shows the number of different types of cakes a bakery baked at different times of a particular day.

At 7:00 am : 15 chocolate cakes, 20 lemon cakes and 12 vanilla cakes.

At 10:00 am : 20 chocolate cakes, 40 lemon cakes and 15 vanilla cakes.

At 1:00 pm : 10 chocolate cakes, 30 lemon cakes and 25 vanilla cakes.

At 4:00 pm : 12 chocolate cakes, 15 lemon cakes and 45 vanilla cakes.

At 7:00 pm : 10 chocolate cakes, 25 lemon cakes and 20 vanilla cakes.

Complete the table to show the given data.

Time	Number of cakes baked			Total number of cakes
	Chocolate	Lemon	Vanilla	
7:00 am				
10:00 am				
1:00 pm				
4:00 pm				
7:00 pm				
Total				

(a) Which is the most popular type of cake? _____

(b) At which time was the most number of cakes baked? _____

(c) How many cakes did the bakery bake in all? _____

(d) If chocolate cakes were charged at $4 each, lemon cakes at $5 each and vanilla cakes at $6 each, how much did the bakery collect from the sale of all the cakes that day? _____

20. The data below shows the number of different types of coins in Amy's piggy bank in the years 1996 to 2001.

1996 : 25 half-dollars, 30 quarters, 45 dimes, 96 nickels and 50 pennies.

1997 : 34 half-dollars, 15 quarters, 40 dimes, 98 nickels and 15 pennies.

1998 : 40 half-dollars, 22 quarters, 16 dimes, 106 nickels and 85 pennies.

1999 : 60 half-dollars, 25 quarters, 46 dimes, 81 nickels and 12 pennies.

2000 : 88 half-dollars, 5 quarters, 40 dimes, 6 nickels and 5 pennies.

2001 : 19 half-dollars, 108 quarters, 11 dimes, 98 nickels and 85 pennies.

Complete the table below to show the given data.

Year	Number of coins				
	Half-Dollars	Quarters	Dimes	Nickels	Pennies
1996					
1997					
1998					
1999					
2000					
2001					
Total					

(a) In which year did Amy have the most number of dimes? _____

(b) How much more money did Amy save in the year 2000 than in 1999? _____

(c) In which years did Amy save the same amount of money? _____

(d) How much did Amy save in all the six years? _____

Topic 5: Angles

1. In each figure, write down the number of angles which are smaller than 90°. Mark these angles.

(a)

☐

(b)

☐

(c)

☐

(d)

☐

(e)

☐

(f)

☐

71

2. Study the figures. Then write down the number of right angles in each figure. Mark these angles.

(a)

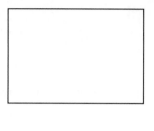

(b)

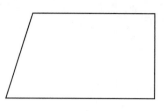

(c)

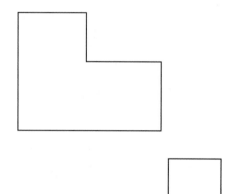

(d)

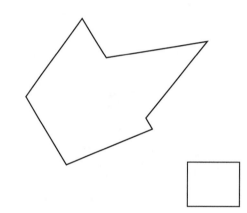

(e)

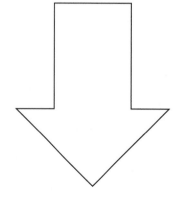

(f)

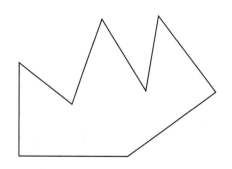

3. In each figure, write down the number of angles which are greater than 90°. Mark these angles.

(a)

(b)

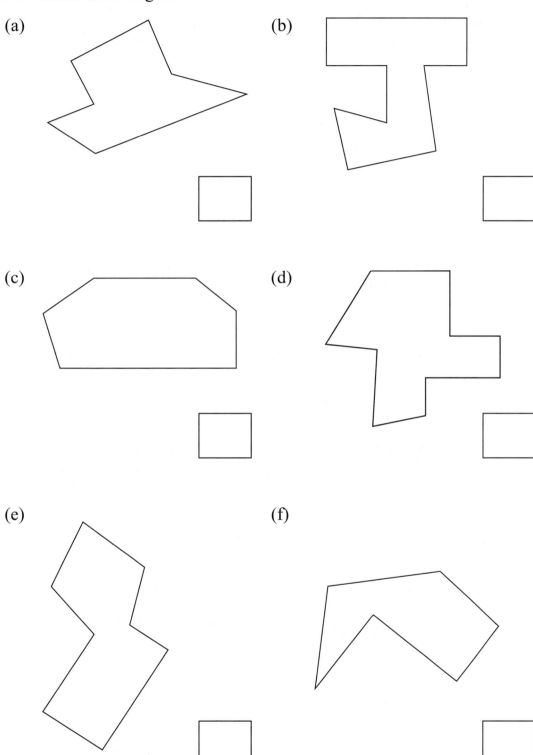

(c)

(d)

(e)

(f)

4. The following angles are smaller than 90°. Measure and write down the size of each angle.

(a)

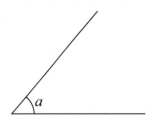

∠a = ☐

(b)

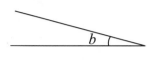

∠b = ☐

(c)

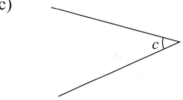

∠c = ☐

(d)

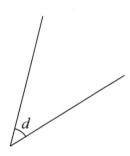

∠d = ☐

(e)

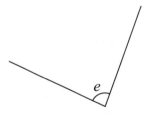

∠e = ☐

(f)

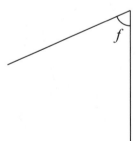

∠f = ☐

5. Estimate and then measure the size of the marked angle in each figure.

(a)

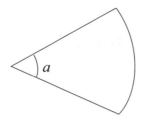

Estimate: _____

∠a = [ ]

(b)

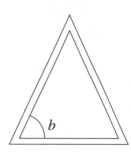

Estimate: _____

∠b = [ ]

(c)

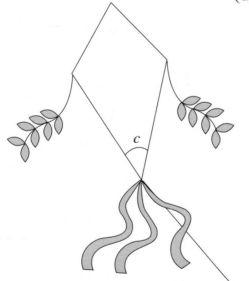

Estimate: _____

∠c = [ ]

(d)

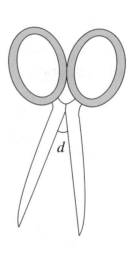

Estimate: _____

∠d = [ ]

(e)

Estimate: _____

$\angle e = $ ▢

(f)

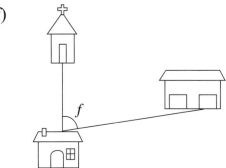

Estimate: _____

$\angle f = $ ▢

6. The following angles are greater than 90°. Measure and write down the size of each angle.

(a)

$\angle a = $ ▢

(b)

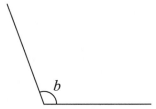

$\angle b = $ ▢

(c)

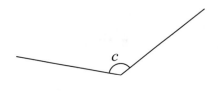

$\angle c = $ ▢

(d)

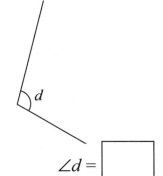

$\angle d = $ ▢

76

(e)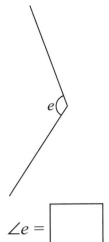

e

$\angle e = \boxed{}$

(f)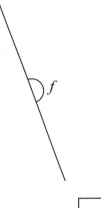

f

$\angle f = \boxed{}$

7. Estimate and then measure the size of the marked angle in each figure.

(a)

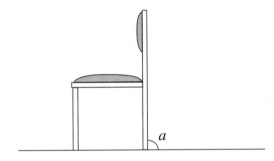

a

Estimate: _____

$\angle a = \boxed{}$

(b)

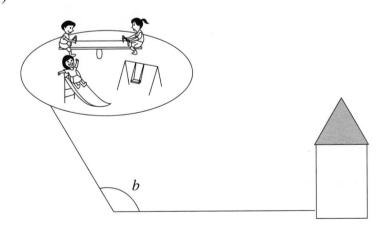

b

Estimate: _____

$\angle b = \boxed{}$

(c)

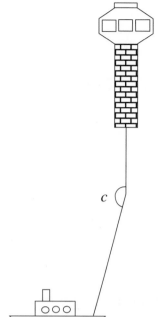

Estimate: _____

$\angle c = $ ☐

(d)

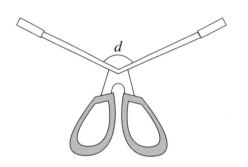

Estimate: _____

$\angle d = $ ☐

(e)

Estimate: _____

$\angle e = $ ☐

(f)

Estimate: _____

$\angle f =$ ☐

8. The following circles are divided into 4 equal parts each. In each circle, follow the turning arrow and write down the size of the angle marked by it. Then write down the number of right angles represented by the turning arrow.

(a)

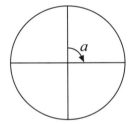

$\angle a \ =$ ☐

$\quad\ =$ ☐ right angle

(b)

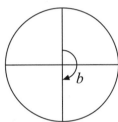

$\angle b \ =$ ☐

$\quad\ =$ ☐ right angles

(c)

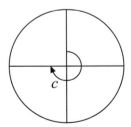

$\angle c \ =$ ☐

$\quad\ =$ ☐ right angles

(d)

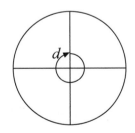

$\angle d \ =$ ☐

$\quad\ =$ ☐ right angles

9. Using the marked end point of each line, draw the required angle in the space given. Then mark the angle. The first one has been done for you.

(a)

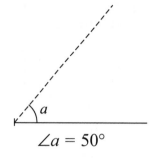

$\angle a = 50°$

(b)

$\angle b = 35°$

(c)

$\angle c = 90°$

(d)

$\angle d = 63°$

(e)

$\angle e = 19°$

(f)

$\angle f = 81°$

10. Using the marked end point of each line, draw the required angle in the space given. Then mark the angle. The first one has been done for you.

(a)

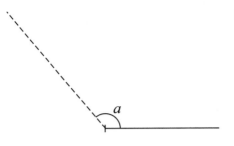

$\angle a = 130°$

(b)

$\angle b = 115°$

(c)

$\angle c = 146°$

(d)

$\angle d = 164°$

(e)

$\angle e = 102°$

(f)

$\angle f = 177°$

11. Draw an angle equal to 68°.

12. Draw an angle equal to 23°.

13. Draw an angle equal to 84°.

14. Draw an angle equal to 31°.

15. Draw an angle equal to 147°.

16. Draw an angle equal to 171°.

17. Draw an angle equal to 92°.

18. Draw an angle equal to 123°.

19. Find the unknown marked angle in each of the following figures.

(a)

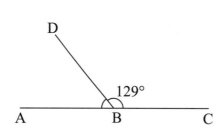

∠ABD = ☐

(b)

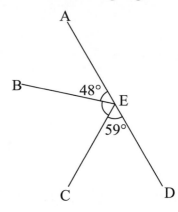

∠BEC = ☐

(c)

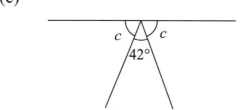

∠c = ☐

(d)

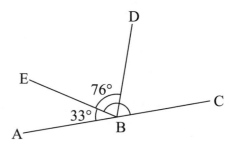

∠EBC = ☐

(e)

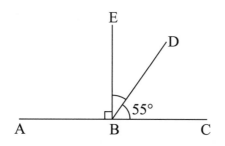

∠EBD = ☐

(f)

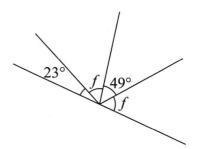

∠f = ☐

20. Find the unknown marked angle in each of the following rectangles.

(a)

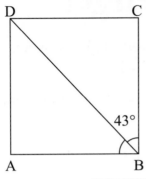

∠ABD = ☐

(b)

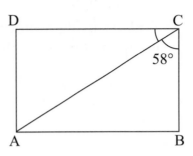

∠ACD = ☐

(c)

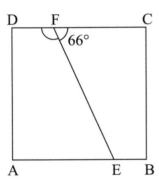

∠DFE = ☐

(d)

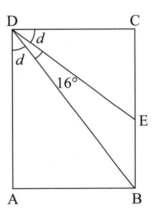

∠d = ☐

(e)

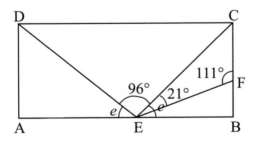

(i) ∠e = ☐

(ii) ∠FEB = ☐

(iii) ∠BFE + ∠FBE + ∠FEB = ☐

Take the Challenge!

1. Without using a protractor, find the marked angle between the hour and minute hands on each of the following clocks.

Clue: The angle between the hour hand and the minute hand is 90°.
Hence, $\angle m = 90°$.

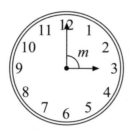

(a)

$\angle a =$ ☐

(b)

$\angle b =$ ☐

(c)

$\angle c =$ ☐

(d)

$\angle d =$ ☐

2. With the minute hand given on each of the following clocks, draw the hour hand to show the required angle. Then mark the angle.

(a)

∠A = 180°

(b)

∠B = 240°

(c)

∠C = 300°

(d)

∠D = 0°

3. How many right angles are there on all the faces of a cube as shown below?

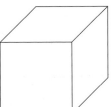

There are ☐ right angles on all the faces of the cube.

4. Fill in the box in each of the following.

(a)

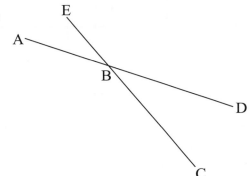

∠ABC = 159°

∠EBA + ∠DBC = ☐

(b)

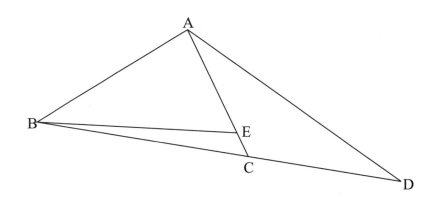

The size of ∠PQR is eight times the size of ∠SQR.

∠PQT + ∠RQS = ☐

5. Look at the figure. List all the angles smaller than 90° in Table A and all the angles greater than 90° in Table B. (Exclude angles which are 180°)

Table A	
∠BAE	

Table B	
∠BAD	

6. It is now 3 o'clock. When the time is 6 o'clock, the hour hand would have made a $\frac{1}{4}$-turn on the face of the clock. How many $\frac{1}{4}$-turns does the hour hand make in 1 day?

The hour hand makes ⬚ $\frac{1}{4}$-turns in 1 day.

7. In the figure, ABCD is a rectangle and ∠GDE is a right angle.

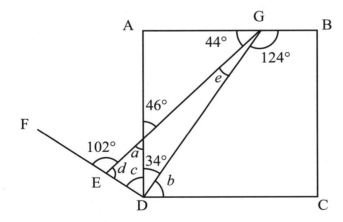

(a) ∠b + ∠c = ⬚

(b) ∠b + ∠e = ⬚

(c) ∠e + ∠c = ⬚

(d) ∠a + ∠b = ⬚

(e) ∠a + ∠c + ∠d = ⬚

1. Identify all the pairs of perpendicular lines by using a set-square or a protractor. Then circle them.

(a)
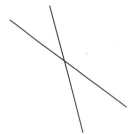

(b)
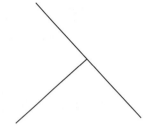

(c)
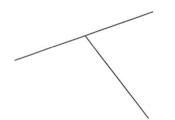

(d)
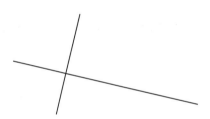

(e)
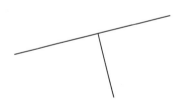

(f)
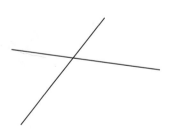

(g)
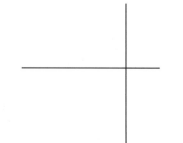

(h)

2. In each of the following figures, name each pair of perpendicular lines. The first one has been done for you.

(a)

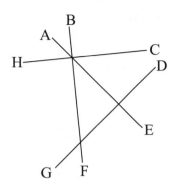

BG ⊥ AD

HE ⊥ BG

(b)

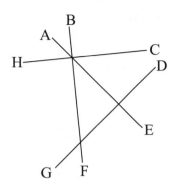

(c)

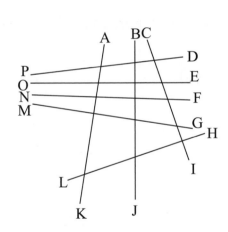

(d)

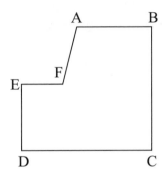

(e)

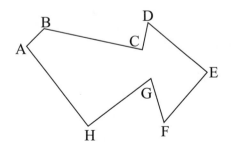

(f)

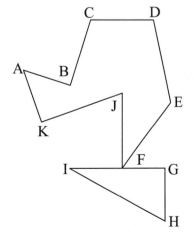

(g)

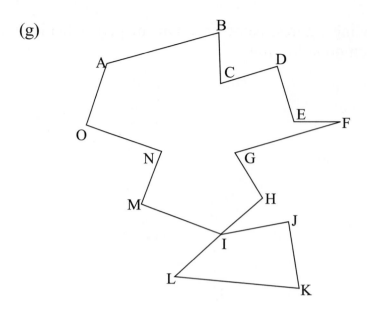

3. Using a set-square and a ruler, draw a line perpendicular to each of the following lines.

(a)

(b)

(c)

(d)

(e)

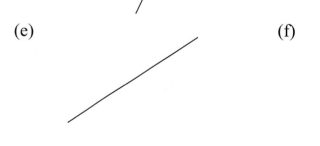

(f)

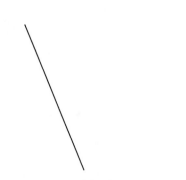

(g) 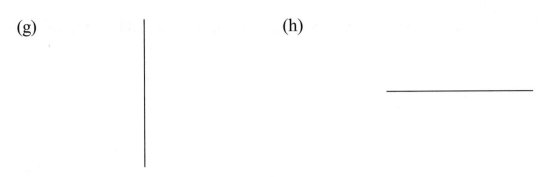 (h)

4. Using a set-square and a ruler, draw a line perpendicular to each of the following lines through the point O.

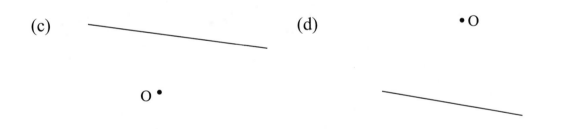

(a)   O•

(b)   •O

(c)

(d)   •O

     O•

(e)

     •O

(f)

     • O

(g)

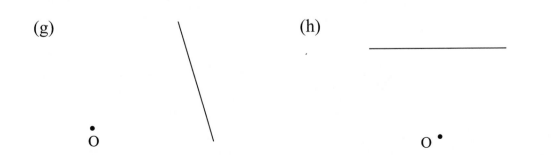

(h)

     •
     O

     O •

5. Using a ruler only, draw a line perpendicular to each of the following lines.

(a)

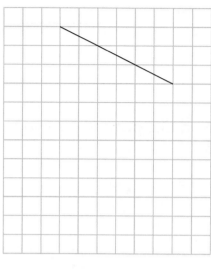

(b)

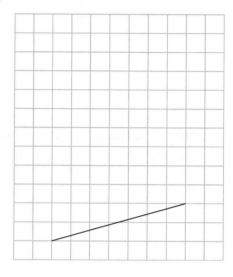

(c)

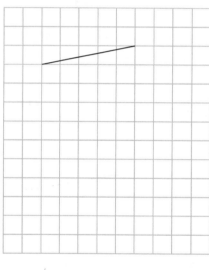

(d)

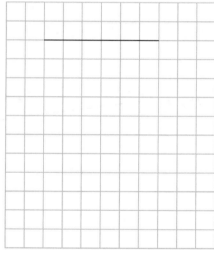

(e)

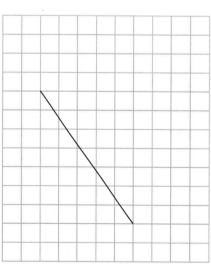

(f)

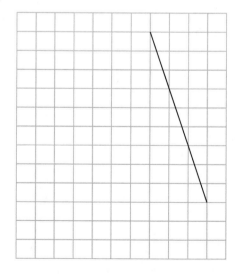

6. Identify all the pairs of parallel lines by using a set-square and a ruler. Then circle them.

(a)

(b)

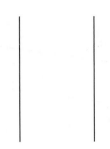

(c)

(d)

(e)

(f)

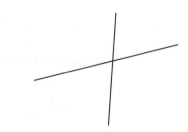

(g)

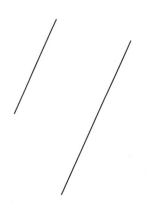

(h)

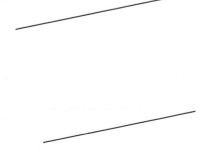

7. In each of the following figures, name each pair of parallel lines. The first one has been done for you.

(a)

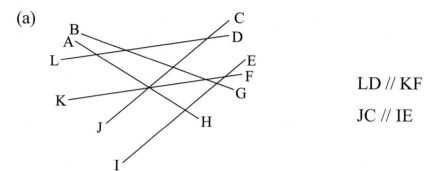

LD // KF

JC // IE

(b)

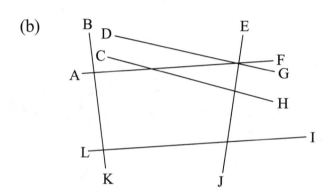

(c)

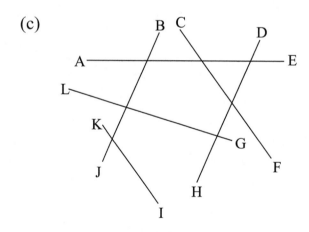

(d)

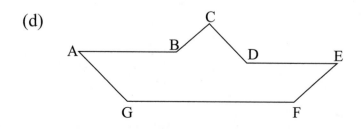

(e)

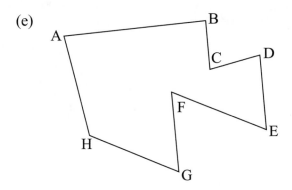

(f)

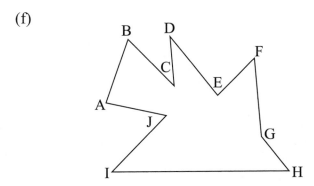

(g)

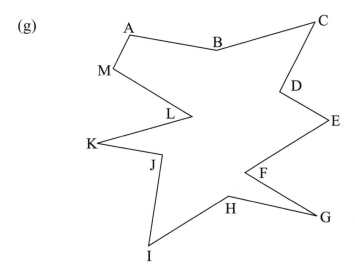

8. Using a set-square and a ruler, draw a line parallel to each of the following lines.

(a)   (b)

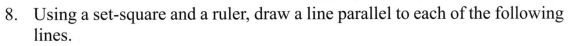

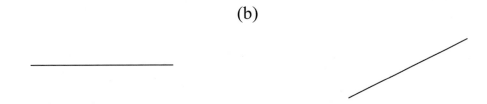

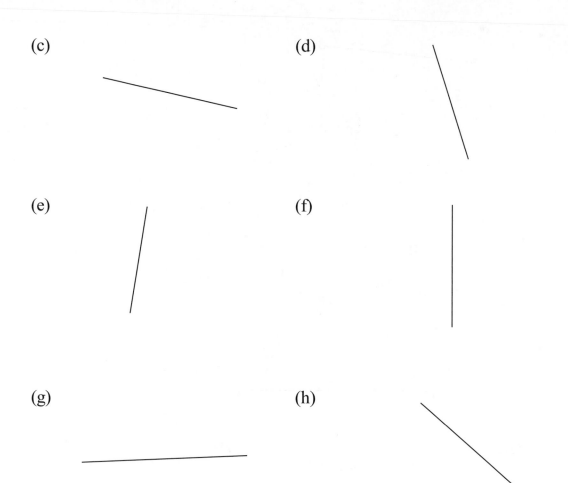

(c)

(d)

(e)

(f)

(g)

(h)

9. Using a set-square and a ruler, draw a line parallel to each of the following lines through the point A.

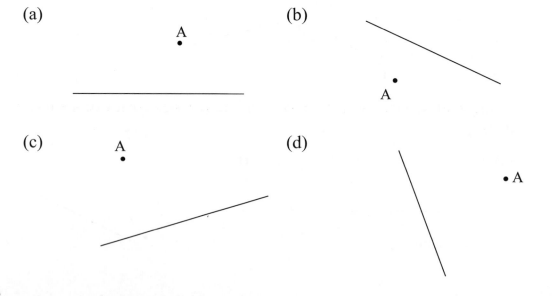

(a)

A

(b)

A

(c)

A

(d)

• A

(e) _____ (f)

(g) 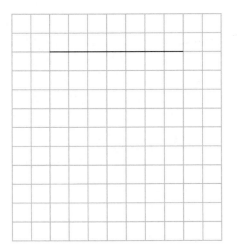 (h)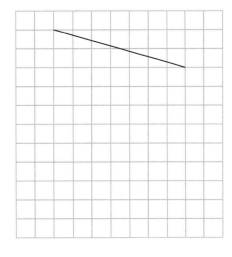

10. Using a ruler only, draw a line parallel to each of the following lines.

(a) 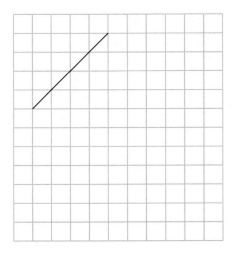 (b)

(c) (d)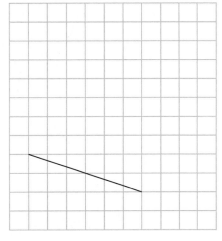

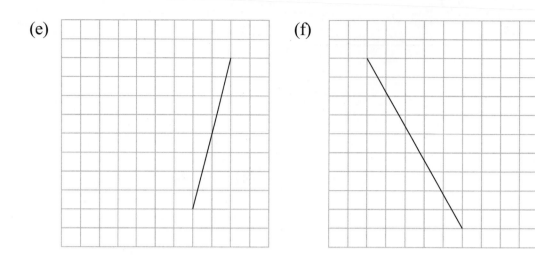

(e)   (f)

11. List all the pairs of perpendicular lines and all the pairs of parallel lines in the table below.

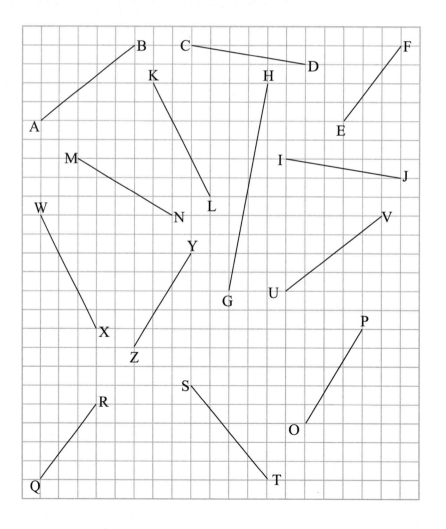

Perpendicular lines	Parallel lines

Take the Challenge!

1. Using a set-square and a ruler, draw a pair of parallel lines such that one line passes through point P and the other line passes through point Q.

P•

• Q

2. Using a set-square and a ruler, draw a pair of perpendicular lines such that one line passes through point P and the other line passes through point Q.

P •

•
Q

3. Look at the figure.

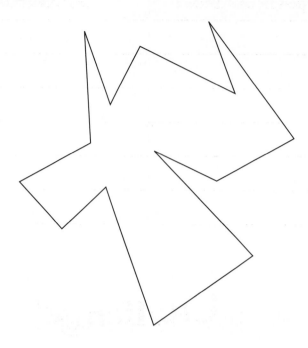

(a) How many pairs of parallel lines are there? _____

(b) How many pairs of perpendicular lines are there? _____

4. Fill in the blanks with the words 'vertical' or 'horizontal'.

(a) A _____ line and a _____ line form a
pair of perpendicular lines.

(b) A _____ line and a _____ line form a
pair of parallel lines.

5. How many letters of the alphabet have at least one pair of

(a) parallel lines,

(b) perpendicular lines?

1. Find the perimeter and area of the following figures.

(a)
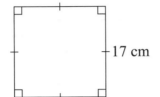
17 cm

(b)
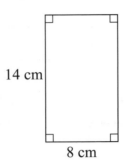
14 cm
8 cm

(c)
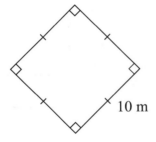
10 m

(d)
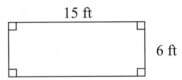
15 ft
6 ft

(e)
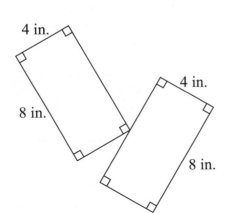
4 in.
8 in.
4 in.
8 in.

(f)
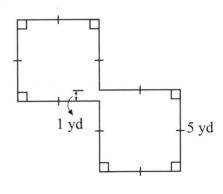
1 yd
5 yd

2. Find the perimeter of each of the following marked figures.

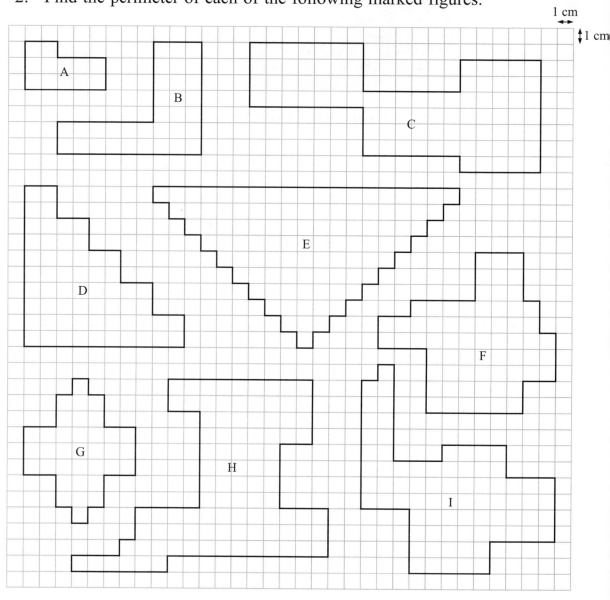

Figure	Perimeter
A	
B	
C	
D	
E	

Figure	Perimeter
F	
G	
H	
I	

3. Find the area of each of the following marked figures.

1 cm
1 cm

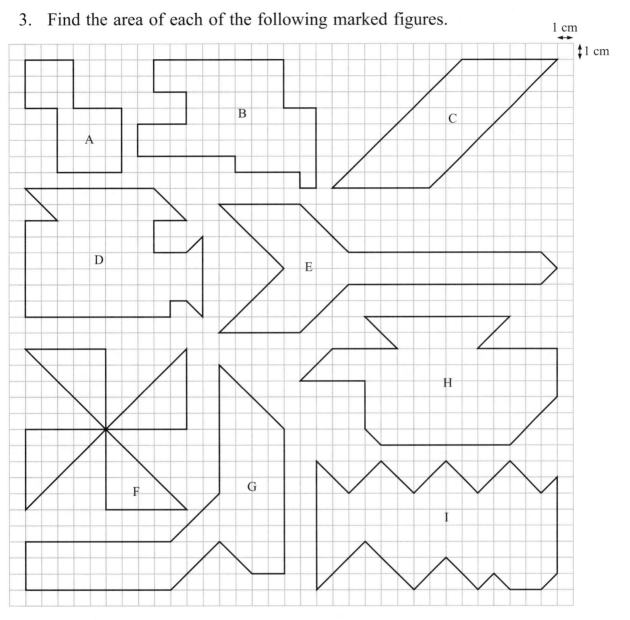

Figure	Area
A	
B	
C	
D	
E	

Figure	Area
F	
G	
H	
I	

4. Find the perimeter of each of the following figures.

(a)
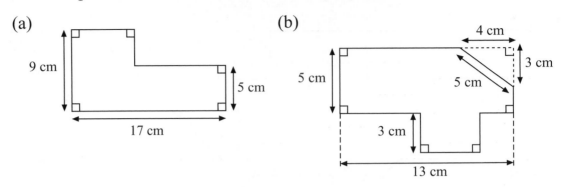

(b)

(c)
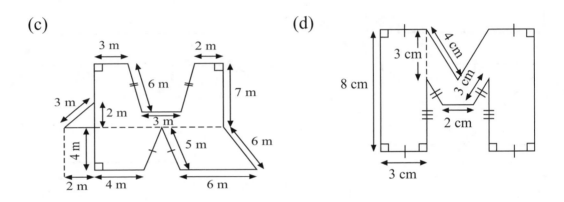

(d)

(e)
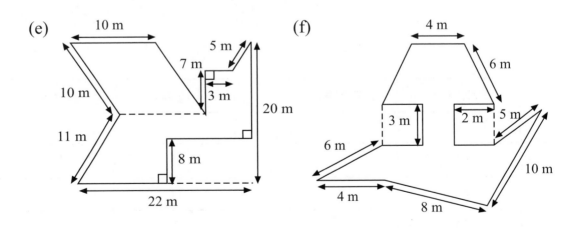

(f)

106

5. Find the area of each of the following figures.

(a)

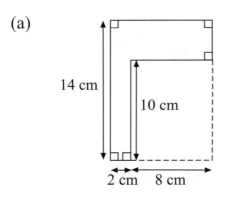

(b)

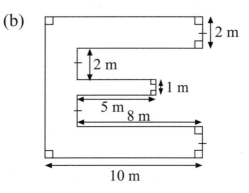

(c)

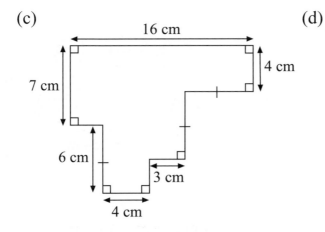

(d)

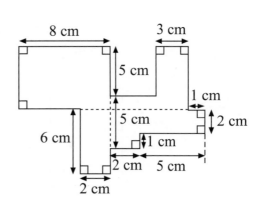

(e)

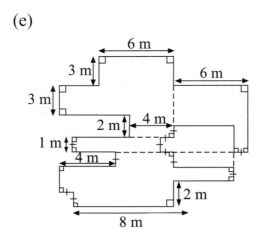

(f)

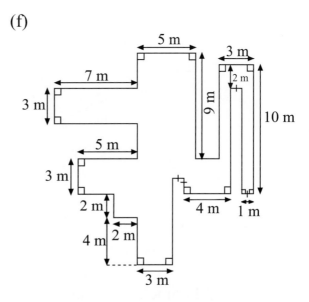

6. Using the given information, find the area of each of the following figures.

(a)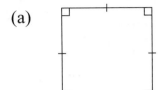

Perimeter = 36 cm

(b)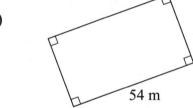

13 cm

Perimeter = 50 cm

(c)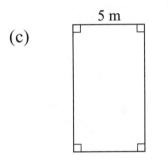

5 m

Perimeter = 62 m

(d)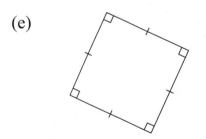

54 m

Perimeter = 140 m

(e)

Perimeter = 72 in.

(f)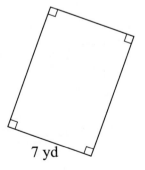

7 yd

Perimeter = 32 yd

7. Using the given information, find the perimeter of each of the following figures.

(a)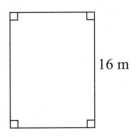

16 m

Area = 64 m²

(b)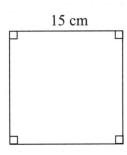

15 cm

Area = 225 cm²

(c)

7 cm

Area = 112 cm²

(d)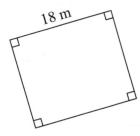

18 m

Area = 270 m²

(e)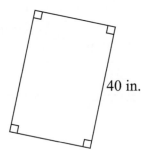

40 in.

Area = 1000 in.²

(f)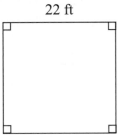

22 ft

Area = 484 ft²

8. Find the unknown marked length in each of the following figures.

(a)

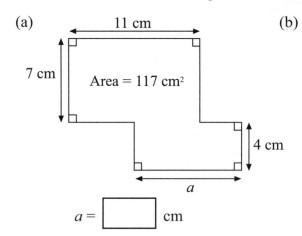

$a =$ [   ] cm

(b)

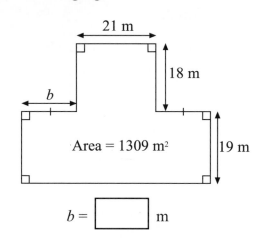

$b =$ [   ] m

(c)

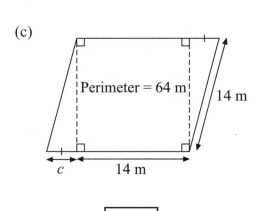

$c =$ [   ] m

(d)

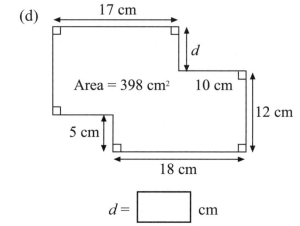

$d =$ [   ] cm

(e)

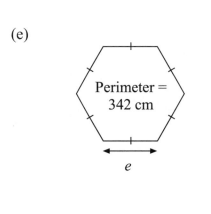

$e =$ [   ] cm

(f)

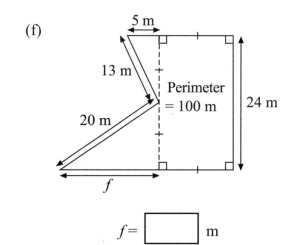

$f =$ [   ] m

9. Find the area of the shaded part in each of the following figures.

(a)

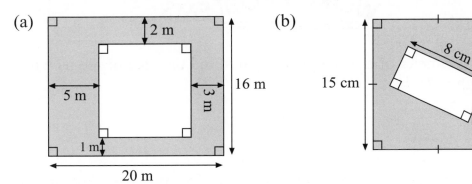

(b)

(c)

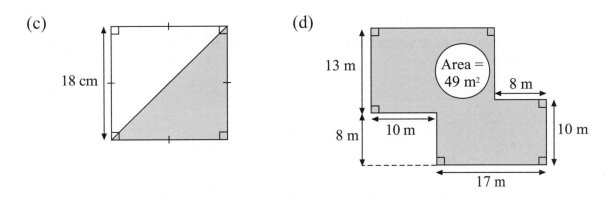

(d)

(e)

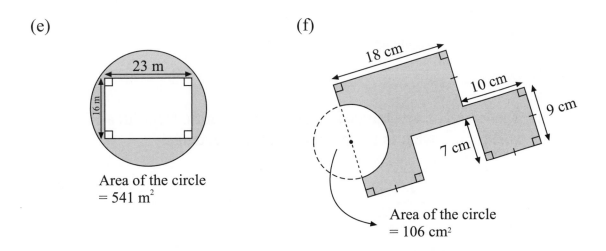

(f)

WORD PROBLEMS

1. The perimeter of a rectangle is 48 in. Find the area of the rectangle if its length is 16 in.

2. A rectangular picture measures 82 cm by 75 cm. It has a border 7 cm wide around it. What is the area of the border?

3. The area of a square plot of land is 256 ft^2. What is the perimeter of the plot of land?

4. The perimeter of a square has a value which is equal to that of its area. What is the length of the square, in centimeters?

5. The length of a rectangle is four times its width. If the area of the rectangle is 196 cm^2, what is the perimeter of the rectangle?

6. The perimeter of a rectangular room is 60 yd. Its length is twice its width. It costs $9 to tile 1 yd² of the floor.
   (a) Find the length of the room.
   (b) Find the cost of tiling the floor.

7. Aunt Cecilia wants to paint only the walls and ceiling of her bedroom. The dimensions of each of the four walls and the ceiling are the same. The length of a wall is 8 m and its width is 6 m. The total area of the door and two windows in the room is 24 m². A can of paint can be used to paint an area of 6 m² only. Each can of paint costs $13. If Aunt Cecilia has $500 with her, how much money would she have left after paying for the required number of cans of paint?

8. The diagram shows Gopal's garden. Gopal wants to lay carpet grass in his garden. If it costs $2 per square meter to lay the carpet grass, how much does Gopal have to pay for laying the carpet grass for the entire garden?

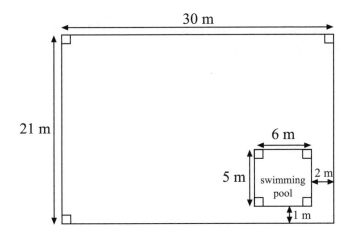

9. The diagram shows Mabel's bedroom. She covers the whole room with carpet except the area where the furniture is. It costs $10 per square meter to lay the carpet. She pays $400 for the laying of carpet. What is the width of her bedroom?

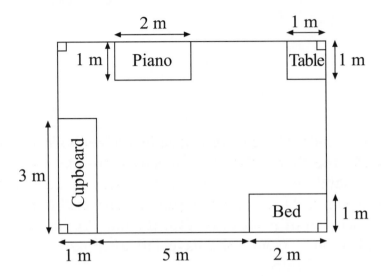

10. A string of length 48 in. is cut into two equal pieces. One piece is used to form a square and the other piece is used to form a rectangle. The length of the rectangle is twice its width. Find
    (a) the area of the square,
    (b) the area of the rectangle.

11. The perimeter of a square has a value which is half that of its area. What is the length of the square, in centimeters?

12. A wall measures 19 ft by 16 ft. How many tiles are needed to cover the wall if the area of every four tiles is 1 ft²?

13. The four corners of a piece of paper have been cut off. The cut-off corners have the same area. What is the area of the remaining piece of paper?

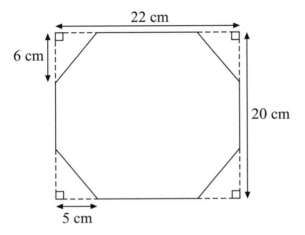

14. The area of the figure is 243 cm². What is the length of AF?

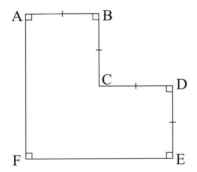

15. The perimeter of Figure A is $\frac{5}{6}$ the perimeter of Figure B. Find the unknown length x.

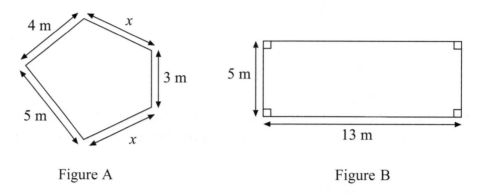

Figure A   Figure B

16. The figure is made up of two squares and a circle. Find the total area of the shaded regions if the area of the circle is 154 cm^2.

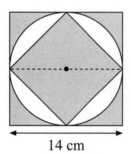

14 cm

17. A field is made up of two equal rectangles, PQRS and TUVW. T is the midpoint of SR. What is the required length of fencing to go around the field?

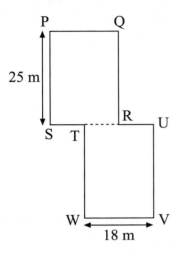

18. The figure is made up of six identical triangles and a rectangle. The lengths of the sides of each triangle are equal. If the perimeter of the figure is 144 cm, what is the area of the rectangle?

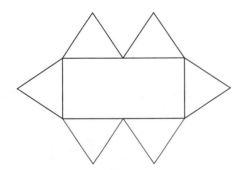

Take the Challenge!

1. A piece of ribbon measures 72 cm by 6 cm. It is then cut along its width into six pieces. Two of the pieces each have a length twice that of each of the other four pieces. What is the total perimeter of the six pieces of ribbon?

2. A coil of wire of length 300 cm is cut and used to form seven rectangles. The length and width of each rectangle formed are each 2 cm longer than the length and width of the previous rectangle. If the first rectangle formed measures 5 cm by 3 cm, find
    (a) the total area of the seven rectangles,
    (b) the length of the wire left after forming the seven rectangles.

3. The figure is made up of a circle and a rectangle. The area and perimeter of the circle are 112 cm² and 36 cm respectively. Find
    (a) the area of the shaded region,
    (b) the perimeter of the shaded region.

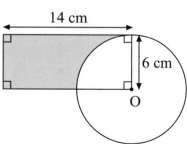

Mid-Year Review

Section A

Four options are given for each question. Only one of them is correct. Choose the correct answer and write its number in the parentheses.

1. In 38,473, the digit 8 stands for _____.
   (1) 8   (2) 80   (3) 800   (4) 8000 (   )

2. When a number is rounded to the nearest hundred, the answer is 72,800. What is the number?
   (1) 71,750   (2) 71,849   (3) 72,750   (4) 73,849 (   )

3. What is the best estimation for 3708 ÷ 9?
   (1) 3600 ÷ 9   (2) 3700 ÷ 10
   (3) 3800 ÷ 9   (4) 3800 ÷ 10   (   )

4. The difference between the 7th multiple of 8 and the 3rd multiple of 12 is _____.
   (1) 20   (2) 36   (3) 56   (4) 92   (   )

5. Find the sum of all the factors of 30.
   (1) 31   (2) 48   (3) 61   (4) 72   (   )

6. Which one of the following numbers does not have 9 as a factor?
   (1) 9   (2) 18   (3) 32   (4) 45   (   )

7. What is the fraction represented by the question mark?

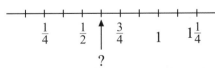

   (1) $\dfrac{2}{3}$ (2) $\dfrac{4}{5}$

   (3) $\dfrac{5}{8}$ (4) $\dfrac{6}{7}$ (   )

8. How many sixths are there in $2\frac{1}{2}$?
   (1) 5   (2) 11   (3) 12   (4) 15   (   )

9. $6 - 3\frac{\square}{4} = 1\frac{1}{2}$

   Find the missing number in the box.
   (1) 1   (2) 2   (3) 4   (4) 6   (   )

10. Fred spent $\frac{3}{5}$ of his pocket money on a movie and lunch. If he had \$20 for his pocket money, how much money did he have left?
    (1) \$4   (2) \$8   (3) \$12   (4) \$15   (   )

11. What fraction of the figure below is **not** shaded?

    (1) $\frac{2}{5}$ (2) $\frac{1}{2}$ (3) $\frac{3}{5}$ (4) $\frac{7}{10}$ (   )

12. Which one of the following has the same value as '$\frac{3}{7}$ of 35'?

    (1) $\frac{1}{2} \times 24$ (2) $\frac{2}{3} \times 30$

    (3) $\frac{3}{8} \times 40$ (4) $\frac{1}{5} \times 55$ (   )

13. Give the sum of $3\frac{2}{3}$ and $\frac{5}{6}$ as a mixed number in its simplest form.

    (1) $2\frac{5}{6}$ (2) $3\frac{5}{6}$

    (3) $4\frac{1}{3}$ (4) $4\frac{1}{2}$ (   )

14. I stand facing you. When I turn around and face you again, how many right angles have I turned through?
    (1) 4   (2) 3
    (3) 2   (4) 1   (   )

15. ABCD and PQRS are squares. How much greater is ∠x than ∠y?

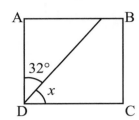 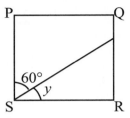

(1) 28°   (2) 88°
(3) 92°   (4) 138°   (   )

16. The time shown on the clock in the figure is 9:20 am. The larger angle formed by the hour and minute hands is between _____.

(1) 0° and 90°
(2) 90° and 180°
(3) 180° and 270°
(4) 270° and 360°   (   )

Refer to the figure below to answer Questions 17 and 18, using a set-square and a ruler.

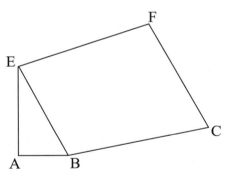

17. Identify a pair of perpendicular lines.
    (1) AF ⊥ EF   (2) EF ⊥ CF
    (3) BE ⊥ BC   (4) AE ⊥ AB   (   )

18. Which one of the following is a pair of parallel lines?
    (1) EF // BC   (2) BE // CF
    (3) AE // CF   (4) AB // BE   (   )

19. PQRS is a rectangle and ST is parallel to RU. How many pairs of parallel lines are there in the figure shown below?

(1)   2
(3)   4
(2)   3
(4)   6   (   )

20. Iris has a piece of wire 120 cm long. She bends it to form a square. What is the area of the square?
(1)   600 cm^2
(3)   1200 cm^2
(2)   900 cm^2
(4)   3600 cm^2 (   )

Section B

Write your answers in the spaces provided.
Answers must be in the units stated.

21. What is the smallest number that can be divided by 3, 6 and 8, without a remainder?

_____

22. How many sixes are there in the product of 3252 and 8?

_____ sixes

23. In the number 16,792, what is the difference between the value of the largest digit and the value of the smallest digit? Round off the answer to the nearest hundred.

_____

24. What number when divided by 8 gives a quotient of 175 and a remainder of 3?

_____

25. A sweater costs twice as much as a shirt. If the total cost of a sweater and 3 shirts is $35, what is the cost of a sweater?

$_____

122

26. List all the common factors of 54 and 81. _____

27. There are 152 books in a class library shelf. $\frac{3}{8}$ of them are Spanish books and the rest are English books. How many English books are there?

_____ English books

28. Arrange the following fractions in decreasing order.

$2\frac{4}{5}, \frac{13}{20}, \frac{2}{5}, \frac{35}{10}$ _____

29. Express 4 months as a fraction of $1\frac{1}{2}$ years. Give the answer in its simplest form.

_____

30. An empty bottle weighs $\frac{1}{6}$ kg. When it is filled with water, it weighs $\frac{1}{2}$ kg. How much does the water weigh? Give the answer in its simplest form.

_____ kg

Study the figure below and use it to answer Questions 31 and 32.
(All lines meet at right angles.)

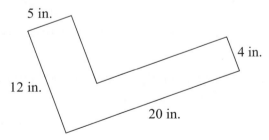

31. Find the perimeter of the figure. _____ in.

32. Calculate the area of the figure. _____ in.²

33. ABC is a straight line. Find ∠x.

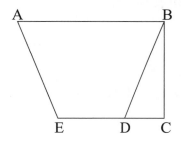

_____ °

34. Which two lines are perpendicular to each other?
(Use a set-square and a ruler to check.)

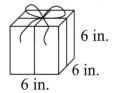

_____

35. A cubical gift box is tied with a piece of ribbon. If the total length of the free ends and the bow is 18 in., what is the length of the ribbon used?

6 in.

6 in.

6 in.

_____ in.

36. Fran jogged round a rectangular field 3 times. If the rectangular field was 120 m long and 75 m wide, what was the distance Fran jogged?

_____ m

37. The length of a rectangle is three times its width. If the length of the rectangle is 48 cm, what is its area?

_____ cm²

38. $\frac{4}{9}$ of the children in a school are boys. There are 1500 girls. What is the total number of children in the school?

_____ children

The table below shows the number of shoppers who bought different brands of toothpaste during a marketing trial. Use the information given in the table below to answer Questions 39 and 40.

Brand	A	B	C	D	E
Number of shoppers	60	90	75	105	40

39. Complete the bar graph below.

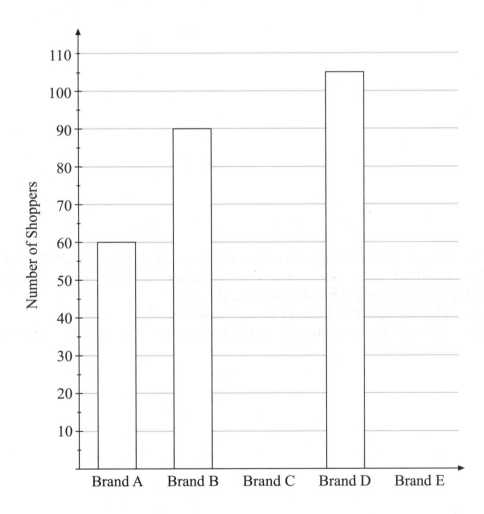

40. If each brand of toothpaste cost $0.80, how much more money was collected for the brand that was most popular compared with the least popular brand?

$_____

Section C

For each question, show your work clearly in the space provided.

41. For every gallon of gas, Mr. Cabby's car can travel 20 mi. He needs to travel 190 mi to reach his destination.
    (a) At least how much gas does he need to pump if he has only 3 gallons of gas left in the fuel tank? Give the answer to the nearest gallon.
    (b) At least how much does it cost Mr. Cabby to refuel his car if each gallon of gas costs $2?

42. The total amount of orange juice in 3 containers, A, B and C, is 2800 ml. Container B has 200 ml more orange juice than container A. There is three times as much orange juice in container C as container B.
    (a) Find the amount of orange juice in container B.
    (b) How much more orange juice is there in container C than in container A?

43. Louisa had $1\frac{5}{6}$ yd of raffia string. Joan also had a piece of raffia string.

After Louisa had given $\frac{2}{3}$ yd of her raffia string to Joan, each of them had an equal length of raffia string. What is the length of Joan's raffia string at first?

44. A square and a rectangle overlap each other as shown.

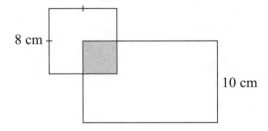

(a) Find the area of the shaded part if it is $\frac{1}{4}$ of the area of the square.

(b) The area of the rectangle is 25 times the area of the shaded part. Find the perimeter of the rectangle, if its width is 10 cm.

45. Sue spent $75 of her money on a few CDs. She spent $\frac{2}{5}$ of the remaining money on books. She then had half of her money left. How much money did she have at first?

More Challenging Problems

1. Observe the pattern in each of the following sets of figures. Draw each missing figure.

(a)   (b)

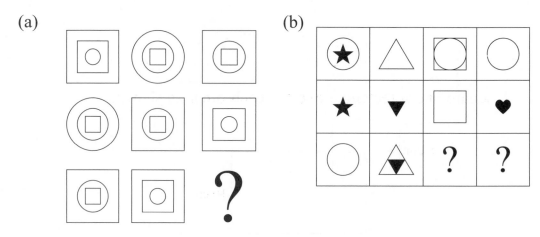

2. The magic square consists of sixteen different numbers from 1 to 16 such that the sum of the four numbers in any horizontal, vertical and diagonal directions is the same. Fill in the missing numbers to complete the magic square.

		7	12
	4	9	
	5	16	3
8	11		

3. The diagram is made up of some squares. Fill in the circles with the numbers 1 to 9 to make the sum of the four numbers at the corners of each square the same. Each number must be used only once.

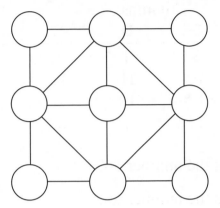

4. Wilson, his wife and his daughter are to be seated on a bench in a studio for a family photograph to be taken. How many photographs can be taken, each with a different seating arrangement?

5. (a) A long piece of rope is 20 m long. If it is to be cut into equal pieces of 5 m each, how many times must it be cut?

   (b) There is a big square pond where six trees are planted on each side. If there is exactly one tree at each corner of the pond, how many trees are planted round the pond altogether?

6. Numbers starting from 1 are arranged in columns below the letters A, B, C, D, E, F and G as shown.

			Columns			
A	B	C	D	E	F	G
1	2	3	4	5	6	7
8	9	10	11	12	13	14
15	16	17	18	...	...	...
...	...	...	...	...	...	...

(a) In which column is the number 54?

(b) In which column is the number 66?

(c) In which column is the number 95?

7. There are two big baskets A and B. Basket A contains 192 apples and basket B contains 24 apples. Each time, 6 apples are removed from basket A and placed in basket B. How many times must this be done so that the two baskets contain the same number of apples each?

8. Uncle Tom sells oranges in a market. On a certain day, he sold half the number of oranges he had and 18 more by noon that day. He then sold half of the remaining ones before he packed up for the day. How many oranges did he have at the beginning of the day if he was left with 26 oranges at the end of the day?

9. (a) Two sticks of lengths 30 cm and 45 cm are tied together as shown.

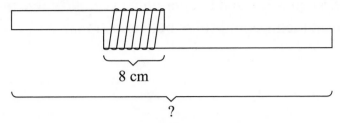

8 cm

?

What is the new length formed?

(b) Two sticks of length 40 cm each are tied together as shown.

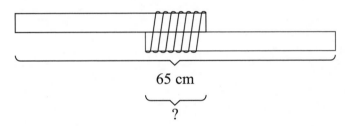

65 cm

?

What is the length of the region tied together?

10. At the Science Museum, a group of fourth graders are lining up to enter the museum. Ben is the 20th student in line and Sam is the 23rd student from the back of the line. Ben is just behind Sam. How many students are there in line?

11. During a math club activity, 18 students were given two interesting questions to solve. Each student could solve at least one question. Ten students could solve the first question and twelve students could solve the second question. How many students could solve both questions?

12. The areas of the rectangular and triangular pieces of paper are 19 cm^2 and 7 cm^2 respectively. They are placed on the table, overlapping each other as shown. Find the area of the overlapping region if they occupy a total area of 21 cm^2 of the table top.

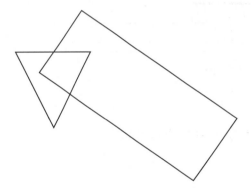

13. On a rectangular piece of land, there are two straight paths which run across the land as shown. The rest of the land is used to grow vegetables. What area of the land is used to grow vegetables?

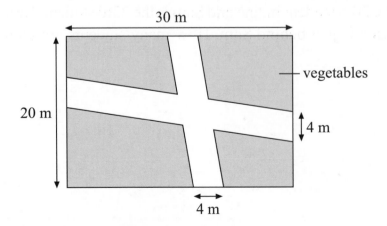

14. ABCD is a square of side 7 cm. E, F, G and H are the mid-points of the sides. What is the area of the shaded part?

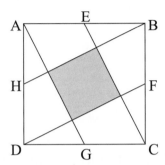

15. From one end of a square piece of paper, a rectangular piece of width 2 cm is being cut off. If the remaining piece of paper has an area of 48 cm², what is the area of the piece of paper being cut off?

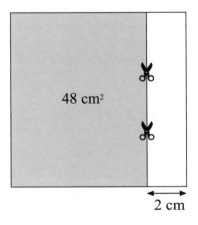

16. The figure shows two squares and a circle. If the area of the big square is 52 cm², what is the area of the small square?

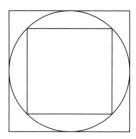

17. ABCD is a square of side 30 cm. E, F, G and H are the mid-points of its sides. I, J, K and L are the mid-points of the sides of the square EFGH. Find the total area of the shaded parts.

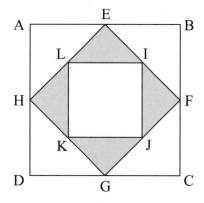

18. Find the value of

$$1 + 2 + 3 + 4 + \ldots + 97 + 98 + 99 + 100.$$